MORE THAN YOU CAN IMAGINE

MORE THAN YOU CAN *Imagine*

WHAT GOD DOES WHEN YOU TRUST HIM

SUSIE LARSON

W Publishing Group

An Imprint of Thomas Nelson

More Than You Can Imagine

Published by W Publishing, an imprint of Thomas Nelson, 501 Nelson Place, Nashville, TN 37214, USA. W Publishing and Thomas Nelson are registered trademarks of HarperCollins Christian Publishing, Inc.

Author represented by The Steve Laube Agency.

Thomas Nelson titles may be purchased in bulk for educational, business, fundraising, or sales promotional use. For information, please email SpecialMarkets@ThomasNelson.com.

ISBN 978-0-7852-9468-9 (SC)
ISBN 978-0-7852-9470-2 (audiobook)
ISBN 978-0-7852-9469-6 (eBook)

Library of Congress Control Number: 9780785294689

Printed in the United States of America

26 27 28 29 30 LBC 5 4 3 2 1

TO JUNIPER GRACE

We've waited so long for you.
Oh, how we love you.
Your precious, miraculous life reminds us to never give up; to keep on praying, believing, and receiving all the best of what God has for us.

TO SCOTT AND WENDY

You are treasured friends and mentors.
Kev and I thank God for you.

SCOTT, *thank you for your ministry to Kev the night before his God-encounter. Truly, you set the stage for him to hear from God. Your wisdom and tender heart mean everything to us. We love you so much.*

No eye has seen, no ear has heard,
and no mind has imagined
what God has prepared
for those who love him.

1 CORINTHIANS 2:9

CONTENTS

FOREWORD

God's way or my way? Trust in myself or in Him alone? Follow the whispers of the Spirit or turn a deaf ear? Believe in the Bible or in my own opinions? Embrace faith or shrink back? Surrender to barriers or trust that God can remove them?

You are about to read a book that can change your life. Wow! Leslie and I are reeling at all we learned as we soaked in the biblical wisdom from these pages. As usual, our friend Susie Larson writes about real life—and unabashedly about our real God. There's hope, she assures us, as we pursue Him even when our path seems littered with impediments.

Leslie and I have seen how the kinds of scriptural principles in this book have carried us through the rough patches of life. When she was a new Christian, Leslie faced the seemingly insurmountable challenge of a husband who was still an adamant atheist. But armed with Scripture and godly friends, she persevered—and she modeled the love of God in a way that pierced even my hardened heart.

Then fresh in my faith, God began leading me to leave the journalism career I had spent years cultivating to take a 60 percent pay cut and accept an obscure role on the staff of a local church. From the world's perspective, it seemed like a demotion. But we trusted the leadings of the Spirit and stepped out into what has become the most wonderful adventure we ever could have imagined.

One day Leslie found me unconscious. She called an ambulance, and when I got to the hospital, I woke up to the doctor's words: "You're one step away from a coma; two steps away from dying." For days I lingered between life and death.

What sustained us during that crisis? The same words from Scripture that calmed our anxiety and bolstered our faith when Leslie was diagnosed with a painful and debilitating neuromuscular condition. God's message of hope, of encouragement, and of unfailing love carried us through that and every other crisis we have faced.

I don't know what turbulent times you might be going through, but I do know where real guidance and strength can be found—and this book will help you find it. You'll thank Susie, as we do, for her passionate and practical teachings about faith.

You are loved, my friend. Rest securely in that. Now turn the page and embark on a spiritual journey that will satisfy your heart, mind, and soul like nothing else.

—Lee (and Leslie!) Strobel

You're Invited . . .

Dear reader, you are someone whom God deeply loves and cherishes. He sees you, knows you, and delights in every detail of your life. I am so grateful to have you along for the journey. I'm praying that as you navigate these pages, you relax your shoulders, open your hands, and breathe in God's abundant grace. Notice the God-moments. Ponder the breakthroughs and consider them possible for you as well. I'm praying these stories stir your faith and awaken a fresh perspective, replacing any limits you impose on yourself or God with eternal possibilities.

No matter where you've been, what you've done, or what's been done to you, God has so much *more* for you—more than you ever imagined! But we seize these treasures one step of faith at a time, often in the context of community. I'm praying God identifies the friends He's appointed for this next leg of the journey. Invite them to join you. I'm praying the words on these pages spark all kinds of conversations about holy expectancy, engaged faith, and a deeper assurance of God's steadfast love. I want everything Jesus won for me. How about you?

I'll be praying for you as you join me on a pilgrimage of faith and expectancy.

God is with us. Right here. Right now.
Great treasures await us.
We're in this together.
Let's be on our way.

AS YOU READ

These words were written with a special rhythm—to invite you in to discover how God has made you for more. The more you dare to trust Him, the more reliable, faithful, and abundantly good you'll find Him to be. Each chapter explores a modern-day story of breakthrough because someone decided to trust God. I'm praying these stories inspire you and activate your faith!

In each chapter you'll also find a story from the Bible that explores people like us who were faced with a choice: Would they trust God or trust themselves? Repeatedly, God's Word shows us how much He wants to be involved in our story. Take your time reading through the chapter content. If you'd like, underline, pray, and highlight what the Lord impresses upon your heart. This is one of the many ways you can start to slow down, listen, and practice the presence of the living God. It's in His presence that you'll better understand who He created you to be. Is there a thought He wants you to take time to ponder? A point He wishes to emphasize? Listen and follow His lead.

Give yourself the time and space to move at the pace of grace. God knows very well what your soul needs in this season. Go slow. Pray through. Take deep breaths when you need them. And listen for the Lord's still, small voice as He whispers fresh revelation to you. Whatever limits you've put on yourself or God, He will gently address so He can lead you to new places of freedom. He will help you uproot whatever lies you've believed about yourself so you're ready for new growth and breakthrough.

At the end of each chapter, I've offered three simple questions for reflection. Give some time and space for those, if you're able. It'll be good for your soul. And for those who love the opportunity for deeper study, you will find personal study questions for each chapter in the back of the book. I'm praying that when you combine the content from these chapters with time in God's Word, your faith will come alive in ways it hasn't before!

And finally, for those who wish to go through this material with their book club, life group, or Bible study, at the back of the book, you'll find group reflection questions. Imagine the kinds of faith conversations you'll have with your friends!

Imagine gathering with your people, leaning in, being honest, and seeking God together. And wonder of all wonders, imagine Him among you, meeting you, whispering His profound truths in your ear, helping you to get free, and changing how you show up in life in the future. That's who He is. That's what He does.

We live in a world that loves to keep us distracted from what matters most. This book is a clarion call to make more space for God, give more airtime to His voice, and engage with His promises because you believe them to be true.

This journey is an invitation to discover who you might become because you dare to trust God and welcome His influence in your life.

I'm praying that after you're done with this book and its questions for reflection, you'll intuitively look around and notice all the ways

God is moving among you. Because He is. I pray, too, that you'll look ahead with hope and expectancy, and faithfully so, because you know in your knower God is actively responding to the faith of His people right now.

I'm praying you'll grow more comfortable in your skin and grow to love the masterpiece God has crafted in you. You're a masterful work in progress!

And finally, I pray that you'll enjoy such rich intimacy with the Lord that listening to His voice becomes the highest priority of your life, and trusting Him feels like the most natural supernatural thing to do. I'm praying you'll be such a bright light in this world that many will ask you what you know.

May the very breath of God fill you, move you, transform you, and make you your truest, most beautiful self.

THE MORE YOU LEARN
TO LIVE INTO THE
MOST TOTAL, MOST
GENUINE SENSE OF
WHO YOU ARE IN
Christ Jesus,
THE MORE
MIRACULOUS YOUR
LIFE WILL BE.

Chapter One

LIVING LOVED

Safety is in God; the people you find there happen to be the people who love and adore him. . . . God's love around us is paired with our choices to love, and that makes for beautiful refuge.

JOHN ELDREDGE,
EXPERIENCE JESUS. REALLY.

And so we know and rely on the love God has for us. God is love. Whoever lives in love lives in God, and God in them.

1 JOHN 4:16 NIV

Maybe you've walked with Jesus for a long time. Or, maybe, you're just meeting Him. Either way, I'm sure you sometimes find yourself thinking, *There's got to be more to this faith journey than what I'm experiencing!* When you read verses that speak of God's power to move mountains, God's love that never fails, and God's desire to be intimately involved in your life, do you ever wonder why your reality rarely feels marked by God's power or reflects such miracle-moving faith? Do you long to see His tangible influence at work in your life?

After years of walking with God, facing down giants, and glaring at some seemingly immovable mountains, I've learned something that's beautifully true: He's still a miracle-working God. He's still the One who parts the waters, who creates beauty out of ashes, and who redeems stories in the most unfathomable ways. And He's still the One in charge. We have the choice as to whether we'll trust Him. And always with significant consequences and outcomes.

Several times in Scripture, we see scenarios where God would have done so much more for His people had they trusted Him, believed Him, and walked in His ways. Consider King Saul, whose story is found in 1 Samuel. He never got out of his own way. He kept making life all about himself. And he missed so much of what God would have done through him. But he's not the only one. Many of the Old Testament kings chose their own way instead of God's. Many of the Old Testament Israelites chose their perspective and preferences ahead of God's. The first generation of emancipated Israelites never even made it to their God-given promised land. However, their children and grandchildren did. What happened? Did God change? No. Their hearts changed. They learned to trust God.

I don't want to miss a thing God wants to tell me, teach me, or do through me. Do you? If God is waiting to expand my understanding of who He is so I can more easily trust Him and live out my kingdom calling during my time on earth, I need His influence. If He is waiting to enlarge my capacity to love the unlovely so I am less rattled by conflict and more purposeful in forgiveness, I need His power. If He wants to move the mountains in my life and change the circumstances that are breaking my heart, I must believe in the power of prayer, persevere when it costs me, and trust that His ways are higher than mine. If God has more for you and me, at some point, we need to trust Him more than we trust ourselves.

I've learned that we lose ourselves when we lose sight of God. When we lose sight of God, we feed our unhealthy appetites because we've lost our spiritual hunger. All our wandering and misplaced affections compel us to magnify our circumstances. We forget who we are when we forget who God is.

Scripture tells us that those who are led by the Spirit of God are children of God (Romans 8:14). How do you know if you're following the Spirit's leadership in your life? The Spirit isn't leading you into despair. That's the Enemy's work. The Spirit isn't forcing you to rehearse your offenses. That's the Enemy's goal. The Spirit isn't baiting you into fearing a future that God isn't part of. That's the Enemy's doing. And remember, he's a liar (John 8:44). We all follow a leader. Is your leader the Enemy's lies? Your negative emotions? Your past painful experiences? Your desire to control all outcomes? Whatever takes up most of your mental space is your leader. What you behold, you become.

Yet when we *magnify* the Lord (focus on who He is above all else until He becomes the biggest, grandest thing in our lives), we begin to see our stories correctly. We reflect our most redeemed selves

> We reflect our most redeemed selves when we get to know God for who He really is and then shift our weight onto His promises because we *know* they're sturdier than our circumstances.

when we get to know God for who He really is and then shift our weight onto His promises because we *know* they're sturdier than our circumstances.

When we build an infrastructure in our hearts and minds that supports God's goodness, faithfulness, and steadfast love, we have more capacity to carry what He assigns to us and more easily reflect His heart for the world. This takes practice, reflection, and application. We set our minds on things above. We imprint God's loving-kindness on our hearts. We repeatedly rehearse the ways He's shown up in our lives. We think so much about His goodness that our intuitive thoughts continually bubble up with expectancy. We wonder what beautifully miraculous thing He'll do next. We continually look for and notice His goodness when it comes. These things don't happen overnight. Nor do they happen without our participation.

Following Jesus, treasuring His presence, counting on His influence, viewing your life through the lens of Scripture, obeying Him when it doesn't suit you, trusting Him when your circumstances scream at you, refusing the Enemy's taunts, accusations, and temptations because you trust God more than your fears—this is what it means to walk with God. The more you know Him for who He truly is, the more you'll absolutely love Him, and the more clearly you'll see yourself as He sees you. When you live loved and called by God Himself, expectancy arises and faith awakens. And miracle of miracles, you start to more clearly see God's involvement in your life in ways you never have before.

IT STARTS WITH SEEING CLEARLY

You know that feeling you get when you're around someone who loves you? Their face brightens when they see you. They laugh because you're hilarious. They notice when you're not okay. They reach out because they love you and want to be with you. You feel loved, safe, and wanted in their presence. They make your life richer. They're who you think of when you've got good news to share and who you want to call when the load feels too heavy to bear.

Those people are gifts from God, wouldn't you say? *They offer glimpses of how God feels about you, times a million.* God thinks about you, cares for you, and is always glad to see you. He enjoys you and appreciates your humor (He gave it to you).

I love to imagine God grabbing His belly, throwing His head back, and laughing out loud at some of the things I say to myself. I love to picture Him leaning in close and whispering correction and redirection when my thoughts lead me into the ditch. It heals my soul to know that God never thinks an unholy thought about me. He truly is my safest place.

How you think about God profoundly affects how you walk with Him. He cares about your dreams, your desires, and your burdens. He's your Creator and your Abba. Your Father and your Friend. You're more loved, covered, and cared for than your precious heart can ever fathom this side of heaven.

To walk in the Spirit is to be deeply acquainted with who God is and how He relates to you. It means knowing and trusting God's love, revering Him as the ultimate authority in your life, and recognizing and trusting His voice when He speaks. Walking intimately with God equips you to navigate life when He seems quiet, never doubting His steadfast, unwavering love. The more you know His heart, the more supernaturally you trust His hand.

He is tender, compassionate, and kind. He is all-knowing, all-powerful, and always good. He is a good Father who disciplines us when we need it, defends us when we're under fire, and rescues us when we're in over our heads. Everything He does in us and for us is for our good and for His glory.

LIVING JUDGED

Now think about how you feel around someone who barely tolerates you. The qualities that many people love about you, they find disdainful. Those beautiful attributes that others celebrate, they berate. They can't see you for the magnificent creation you are. They see through a skewed lens that distorts all that's right and remarkable about you. And the messy parts of you that are still in process? Where God is tender, patient, and kind with your weaknesses, they are harsh, impatient, and flippant regarding your healing process. You're not safe with them. They've assessed you, made judgments about you, and there's no changing their minds. You're not your best self when you're around them. You're a stunted, edited version of yourself, and you know it's not good or right.

I've often wondered why God allows people like this into our lives, but now I know how powerfully their sharp edges soften mine. And how deeply I sense the Father's love in contrast to their hurtful ways. Furthermore, these people also give you a glimpse into the eternal realm. Here you see a bit of how the Enemy feels about you—times a million. He's threatened by you, hates you, and is terrified at the thought of you breaking free from his grip. So he perpetually hits you where it hurts most—until you learn to walk by the Spirit and put his hurtful, harmful ways under your feet.

Have you ever noticed that when you live loved, when God's Word is alive in you and His Spirit leads the way in and through you, that you're downright brilliant? Your capacity for fruitfulness increases exponentially. You offer wise insights that you never could have come up with on your own. You discern issues without needing to know every detail. You see with eyes of faith and know intuitively that there's more to the story than what your earthly eyes see. When you walk in the Spirit, you speak with precision and pray with power. You live an otherworldly life.

Have you also noticed that when you're in the flesh (negatively self-aware, reacting to other people's junk, overwhelmed by your fears, and so on), you're your most awkward, graceless self? Well, maybe it's different for you, but let me speak for myself. I'm my most bumbling self when I'm walking in the flesh.

Scripture reminds us that when our thoughts are Spirit-fueled and Spirit-led, our lives will be marked by the peace and power of God. We'll know what to do and when to do it. What to say, and when to say it. How to think and how to pray. But this takes intention. We don't often default to a faith perspective. We more instinctively gravitate toward thoughts of fear, discouragement, or disappointment. We need the Spirit of God to show us how to know and rely on the love of God; how to walk in the power of God.

> Now the mind of the flesh is death [both now and forever—because it pursues sin]; but the mind of the Spirit is life and peace [the spiritual well-being that comes from walking with God—both now and forever]. (Romans 8:6 AMP)

YOUR BEST SELF IS HIDDEN IN CHRIST

We're not alone. Every saint who has gone before us has wrestled with the battle between the flesh and the Spirit. Every saint has been tempted to trust themselves more than they trust God. This is not a

PAUSE.

BREATHE.

PONDER.

Who in your life has loved you well?

In what ways has their love healed, strengthened, or reassured you?

new struggle. When King Saul was anointed by God, he prophesied and was a mighty warrior. When he got in his head, walked in the flesh, and decided to make it all about himself, he hid behind his baggage, took credit that belonged to God alone, and tried to kill God's next appointed king. In the Spirit, King Saul was mighty. On his own, he was a bumble head.

When King David operated in the flesh, he made deadly and devastating mistakes, impacting many lives. When he walked by the Spirit, he was a brilliant king, a worshiping warrior, and a stunning prophet.

Your best, most profoundly redeemed self is *hidden in Christ.* Christ *in you* is your hope of glory (Colossians 1:27). When you see Jesus for who He really is, you see yourself as God sees you. And what He sees, He absolutely loves. If you could see what God sees when He looks at you, your days of feeling insecure would become few and far between.

I submit that we will never fully understand who we are in Christ apart from deeper and growing revelations about who God is. Our value does not increase the more we understand or believe it, but its truth undoubtedly influences how we show up in life and what others encounter when they meet us. If our value is an ocean, most of us hold only a Dixie cup.

Have you stopped lately to consider what Jesus won for you? He tore the veil in two! You can come boldly into the throne room of almighty God, fully assured that He's always glad to see you! Because of Jesus, God has gifted you with spiritual eyes to see and discern all the ways He's moving on the earth. He's grafted you into the royal family line and covered you with His promises. You couldn't be more secure than seated with Christ, as the Scriptures say (Ephesians 2:6). And since you've been given access to know God intimately, you've also been granted the privilege of reflecting Him miraculously to a world that so desperately needs Him. As you and I *see and reflect* God's glory, we are changed, miraculously so, from the inside out.

> But whenever someone turns to the Lord, the veil is taken away. For the Lord is the Spirit, and wherever the Spirit of the Lord is, there is freedom. So all of us who have had that veil removed can see and reflect the glory of the Lord. And the Lord—who is the Spirit—makes us more and more like him as we are changed into his glorious image. (2 Corinthians 3:16–18)

If you struggle with fixating on your circumstances, forgetting God's promises, and defaulting to regular bouts of insecurity, know this: God has so much *more* for you! If you long to be awakened to all the ways God is moving in your life, join us on this journey. If you've been praying for a personal revival, this book is for you. Your choices, your gaze, your faith, and your trust all matter deeply to God, and all affect how your story unfolds.

Each day, we have multiple opportunities to draw on the living Spirit of God within us or to default to our flesh, which always leads to destruction. We possess agency in the kingdom! We have God's Spirit! We have His promises. May we awaken to all that God has made available to us. A. W. Tozer wrote:

> A spiritual kingdom lies all about us, enclosing us, embracing us, altogether within reach of our inner selves, waiting for us to recognize it. God Himself is here waiting for our response to His Presence. This eternal world will come alive to us the moment we begin to reckon upon its reality.[1]

God Himself is here.

He is waiting for our response to His presence.

What if we came alive to the spiritual world all around us? What if we awakened to the reality of Christ within us? What if we allowed the Spirit more access to our thoughts, dreams, and tendencies to self-protect?

I'll tell you what will happen. We'll finally travel light; we will be flexible in the moment to move with the Spirit and enjoy one divine surprise after another. The Bible says that where the Spirit of the Lord is, there is liberty (2 Corinthians 3:17). And that the Spirit of the living God *leads us into all truth* (John 16:13).

Freedom and truth. Isn't that what we need right now? Far too many people are held captive by lies. They're far from free. Yet God invites and calls us to freedom, healing, and wholeness.

In the chapters ahead, we will search the Scriptures for examples of how God's appointed people moved in and out of their true identities, how their biggest mistakes occurred when they forgot who they were, and how, in His mercy, God is always there, ready to forgive and redeem. Even so, there is a significant cost when we forget who we are and fear rules the day.

It matters that you grow in the knowledge of God. You must understand who you are because of who God is. It's essential to rely on the Holy Spirit. And the more you learn to live into the most total, most genuine sense of who you are in Christ Jesus, the more miraculous your life will be.

Let's journey together to identify and overcome our fears more quickly and become more sensitive to the Holy Spirit's influence. Let's ask God to awaken us to His love and power and transform us into people we never dreamed we could be. God is more than willing to answer those prayers. May God awaken you, heal you, free you, and activate you in ways you never dreamed possible.

PRAYER

Precious Father,

I want to know You more. Awaken my heart. Open my ears. Stir up my faith! Too often, I base my view of You on my past experiences or my current circumstances. It's so easy to live an earthbound life. I want to walk in Your presence as I live here on earth.

Open my eyes to notice the people in my life who love me well. I never want to take them for granted. May their love make Your love more believable. Help me to see those You've given me to love. May I reflect Your heart to them.

Show me the moments when I'm not walking in the Spirit. Be quick to convict me and lead me back to the path of life. Fill me afresh today with Your Spirit, and awaken me anew to Your divine purposes for me.

Amen.

MOMENTS OF REFLECTION

1. Read Romans 5:5 and dare to take this verse literally. Imagine God pouring a fresh dose of love into your heart and that love seeping into the spaces and places where you need a fresh reminder of it. Ask God to bring this passage to life for you.

2. When was the last time you sensed God's love and

slowed down long enough to ponder it and be grateful for it? What did that look and feel like?

3. When you consider all the people Jesus interacted with in the Scriptures, which story most resonates with you? Which interaction most touches your heart?

Chapter Two

GOD GIVES ME PURPOSE AND POWER

We don't have to be strong to be saved. We don't have to be perfect to be redeemed. We don't have to score straight A's. We simply need to trust the God of Jacob, believe in a God who sticks with the unworthy and underachievers until we are safely home.

MAX LUCADO, *GOD NEVER GIVES UP ON YOU*

It is God who arms me with strength and keeps my way secure.
He makes my feet like the feet of a deer; he causes me to stand on the heights.

PSALM 18:32–33 NIV

I shuffled out to my morning prayer spot, grabbed a decaf coffee with almond creamer, heated my cinnamon-scented neck wrap, and snuggled into my favorite prayer nook. I looked at my husband to wish him a good morning before starting my prayer time. I was undone by what I saw. With his head back, eyes closed, and hands resting on his Bible, which lay open on his chest, he tried to control his tears, but his lips quivered as he quietly wept. He didn't look at me, couldn't speak. He was clearly touched by the hand of God.

With my hand over my mouth, I held my breath. I didn't want to disrupt this moment, and yet I wanted in on it. What was God saying to him?

My husband is one of the most capable and competent people I know. He is steady, solid, consistent, and intelligent. He is also gentle, kind, and loving, and he has a deep love for Jesus. He works as a senior project manager, building sports stadiums and large hospitals. Additionally, he serves as a global elder at our church. He mentors young men in the marketplace. Our sons, daughters-in-law, and grandchildren completely adore him.

Yet, for the longest time, he's had a father wound. Deep inside, where most would never notice or even wonder about, lives a core lie that he isn't worth pursuing. He fathers everyone within his sphere of influence so well that you'd never think there was a hole in his own heart.

Kev loved his parents; they were dear, precious people. They are in heaven now. His dad was a quiet, meek, and even passive man. He worked a lot, was rarely available, and didn't actively pursue Kev. These traits were common in that generation. He was faithful to his wife, hardworking, and loved Jesus. Kev would never dare to dishonor his father. Kev is profoundly grateful for growing up in a Christian home. Yet even as an adult, he'd call his dad only to sense his desire to end the conversation quickly to return to his TV show or woodworking. He was a simple man—not engaged, but very kind. However, Kev never felt that his dad had any interest in his life—no input, challenges, or corrections. No pursuit. None whatsoever.

It was hard for Kev to come to grips with the pain buried deep beneath the surface, because he didn't fault his dad in any way. It was just the way things were in those days. But the Lord never leaves us with open wounds. He intends to heal them all. He allows circumstances and situations to stir the pot so that we can see what surfaces.

The Lord never leaves us with open wounds. He intends to heal them all. He allows circumstances and situations to stir the pot so that we can see what surfaces.

This wound showed up at the most unsuspecting times. And Kev hated it. It made him feel weak and vulnerable. But he couldn't deny its presence in his heart. He'd ask himself, *Am I worth pursuing? Worth investing in? Worth fighting for? Worth the time?*

I sat in my little spot on the couch, unable to take my eyes off my husband. This man whom I love so much. This man who had guided me through the fires of hell during my health battles with Lyme disease.

(I'll share more on that later.) Witnessing him tremble and feel undone was almost more than I could bear. I waited quietly and prayed for him. It was a truly sacred moment.

Then, he lifted his head, sat up a little straighter, and, with a cracked voice, gently said, "I've just encountered God." He went on to tell me that he woke up wide-awake at 4:00 a.m. with the strong sense that the Lord wanted to meet with him. Kev went out to his prayer chair, pushed *play* on his worship playlist, rested his head, and closed his eyes.

Suddenly, he felt a palpable sense of God's presence. He didn't move. With startling clarity, Kev became aware of the deep father wound in his heart. But before he could feel vulnerable or exposed, Kev envisioned God's fatherly hand reaching down from heaven and touching that tender spot with immense strength and compassion. Kev held his breath.

He felt God's healing hand on his heart in the most miraculous, tangible way. He felt warmth, love, peace, and an unexplainable sense of God's nearness. With the pressure of His gentle hand still on Kev's heart, the Father whispered, *I'm so sorry, son.* Kev broke down and cried. God's tender compassion undid him. At that very moment, a song from Kev's playlist started to play. A song by Lenny LeBlanc: "There is none like You / No one else can touch my heart like You do."[1]

Kev began to weep, and he couldn't stop. Then, the Lord's voice thundered in his spirit once more. He said, *I need you healed and ready because I'm coming soon. I have things for you to do. I need My people healed and prepared because I have great work for them to do before I return.* I'm hesitant to share this next part, but I will because it was part of Kev's sacred, beautiful experience. After the Lord's charge to Kev, he saw a vision of King Jesus, with the strength of a warrior, looking over His shoulder, pointing and telling an angel, *Go get My horse.*

With both hands over my mouth, I wept too. I couldn't contain it. That God would love my husband so much that He'd intervene in such a tender, healing way? Well, it takes my breath away.

We both needed to get ready for work but couldn't. We sat together for two hours, held hands, cried, and thanked God for His personal, powerful ways with His children.

Something shifted with Kev after that. He suddenly felt a holy urgency to make the days count for eternity. Although he had been fully engaged in the kingdom before this, there was suddenly a power and presence about him that wasn't there before. Kev couldn't talk about that encounter without crying. And if you haven't met him, he's a big, strapping man's man. Not one given to emotional displays.

From that encounter, Kev emerged joyful, tender, in awe, and freshly assured of his Father's love. The things that usually bothered him suddenly became inconsequential. He already had a healthy sense of identity, but this deepened his spiritual root system, forever changing how he walks with God. This fresh revelation of God's fatherly character awakened Kev's understanding of his identity and kingdom call.

How would you respond if God met you in such a way? Would you be undone? Want to run and hide? Wonder if God is mad at you?

Do you know that you're safe in His care? That He loves you with an everlasting love? Do you dare ask Him to show you how He feels about you?

My friend Ann Voskamp writes:

> Look into the eyes of a love that sacrifices for you, that lives to give to you, that surrenders for you, that covers you, that sustains you, that always and unconditionally carries you—and you will commit your life and death to love the same. Here is a place to linger: Jesus

> Christ's love to see you exceeds even your own ache to be seen. His eyes are full of compassion for you—and that compassion is the very passage to complete change within you. Being united with Him is being whole.[2]

One of the worst pains in life is feeling unseen, unknown, unloved. And though the pain is real, the message of rejection is a lie. Jesus came to earth to prove it to you. You're a precious gift to Him. And He's committed to your healing journey. If you'll let Him, He'll lift the layered lies from your heart and replace them with the truth. He's done the hard work. He's paid the ultimate price.

What's yours to do? It's to trust Him. Trust Him when He says He loves you, treasures you, and wants to transform you into someone you never dreamed you could be. Can you picture it? A more healed, healthy version of yourself? Ask God today for a fresh revelation of who He is, and a more truthful perspective of who you are. He loves to answer prayers like that.

WHO IS JESUS? WHO AM I?

Jesus and His disciples stirred up dust on the gravel roads as they approached the region of Caesarea Philippi. Picture the back-and-forth banter, the questions, and stretches of thought-provoking silence.

Suddenly, Jesus turned to His disciples and asked, "Who do people say that the Son of Man is?"

"Well," they replied, "some say John the Baptist, some say Elijah, and others say Jeremiah or one of the other prophets" (Matthew 16:13–14).

Jesus halted the group, and they all gathered around Him. They sensed that another essential lesson was about to unfold. Jesus opened

PAUSE.

BREATHE.

PONDER.

When do you feel most at home in God's presence?

How do you feel about the way God feels about you?

His hands before them and asked, "But who do *you* say I am?" (v. 15, emphasis mine). Look what happened next:

> Simon Peter answered, "You are the Messiah, the Son of the living God."
>
> Jesus replied, "You are blessed, Simon son of John, because my Father in heaven has revealed this to you. You did not learn this from any human being. Now I say to you that you are Peter (which means 'rock'), and upon this rock I will build my church, and all the powers of hell will not conquer it. And I will give you the keys of the Kingdom of Heaven. Whatever you forbid on earth will be forbidden in heaven, and whatever you permit on earth will be permitted in heaven." (vv. 16–19)

Scoot in a little closer and notice what occurred. People who knew and experienced Jesus from a distance had all kinds of ideas about who He *might* be (and the same is true today). But Peter—beautifully imperfect as he was—stayed on Jesus's heels. He followed Him closely and loved Him fiercely. So when Jesus asked the question about His identity, Peter was ready to speak out in faith: "You are the Messiah, the Son of the living God."

Heaven came down and influenced Peter's response. God revealed the truth to Peter about His one and only Son! Peter was chosen to declare this truth aloud. Because Peter received a revelation of who *Jesus* was, he was positioned to better understand who *he* was. Thus, Jesus continued to speak to Peter, addressing not only his identity but also his calling.

Go back and read that passage again, noticing how Jesus addressed Peter's identity and calling. He referred to Peter as a "rock" before Peter ever acted like one. He called out Peter's God-given destiny while it was still in its infancy. Peter was positioned to hear about who he could become because he was postured in faith with an ear turned toward heaven.

My friend Reagan served as a sample reader as I wrote this book. I absolutely love her insight on this moment between Jesus and Peter. Here's what she shared with me:

> How cool was it that Jesus is standing at the gates of hell in Caesarea Philippi by the altar of the god Pan when He says all this in Matthew 16? The disciples knew this was a very demonic area full of pagan worship. Jesus also displayed His ultimate power over the principalities and idols of the world at that moment. He revealed that Peter will have access to this power through the Holy Spirit!

Picture yourself standing there with Jesus in a place of demon worship. Imagine Jesus putting his hands on your shoulders, looking over His shoulder, and then back into your eyes and saying, "The gates of hell will not prevail against My kingdom! Far greater is My Spirit in you than all the demons of hell combined. Soon, I will be alive in you, and you will minister with the authority you've seen in Me." What would you do with such a moment?

Your most authentic self—the one filled with the Holy Spirit, closely following Jesus, addressing the fleshly tendencies He reveals in you, and seeking to know God in ways that transform you forever—is made for a *deeper relationship with God*. You are called to be a vessel of honor, filled with His Spirit, walking in His ways so that you are continually transformed from glory to glory, allowing others to see Him for who He truly is.

You are called to grow in your authority so the gates of hell do not prevail during your time on earth. Maybe you've heard it said, in one way or another, that you have the most authority where you've had your most significant victories. I believe that's true. God wants you to overcome. If you're serious about your relationship with Him, He will teach you how to overcome.

Listen, friend: God loves, cherishes, and accepts you, yes. But He does so much more than that. He pursues you, redeems you, and miraculously transforms you. He's not passive when it comes to you. He's passionate about you! He's actively present with you. He's a miracle-working, soul-restoring, story-redeeming God.

He will love, save, and restore you wherever He finds you. But when you prioritize your proximity to the King, you learn more about His presence, promises, and power. As you gain a deeper understanding of who He is, you *will* receive a more accurate picture of who you are. And when that happens? Everything changes.

As you gain a deeper understanding of who He is, you *will* receive a more accurate picture of who you are. And when that happens? Everything changes.

> See how very much our Father loves us, for he calls us his children, and that is what we are! But the people who belong to this world don't recognize that we are God's children because they don't know him. Dear friends, we are already God's children, but he has not yet shown us what we will be like when Christ appears. But we do know that we will be like him, for we will see him as he really is. And all who have this eager expectation will keep themselves pure, just as he is pure. (1 John 3:1–3)

LIVE FROM A PLACE OF LOVE, NOT FEAR

Here's where the story takes a turn. After Jesus confirmed His identity as the Son of the living God and told the disciples that the gates of hell would not prevail against the church, He began to prepare them for the road ahead. He didn't mince words; He spoke plainly. He needed to go to Jerusalem, where He would suffer greatly at the hands of leading priests and teachers of the religious law. He would be brutally killed, but on the third day, He would rise from the grave, for even death could not stop Him!

Picture those same dusty roads, this jarring conversation. Picture Peter running ahead of Jesus, turning around, stretching out his arms to block Jesus's path, and saying, "Heaven forbid, Lord. . . . This will never happen to you!" (Matthew 16:22).

How did Jesus respond? "Get away from me, Satan! You are a dangerous trap to me. You are seeing things merely from a human point of view, not from God's" (v. 23). If you're wrong about Jesus's identity, you'll be wrong about your own.

By the way, how did this encounter go from a history-making, divine revelation to Peter's fleshly, earthbound reaction in such a short time?

Fear.

Fear binds us, blinds us, and prevents us from seeing things as they truly are. In essence, Jesus said to Peter (and He also says to us), *When you live from a place of fear, you become a dangerous trap to Me. You see things only from a human perspective and not from God's. I must fulfill My destiny so you can fulfill yours. Fear has no place in your heart or your perspective.*

Dr. Rob Reimer writes:

> What you believe about yourself and others will shape how you live. But it isn't enough to have knowledge of the truth; your life must be built upon this foundation of truth, and it must be deeply integrated into your daily existence. This never happens accidentally. You need to build your life on the foundation of who God says you are. This is your identity in Christ, and when this foundation is properly set in your soul, your life can be well constructed.[3]

Jesus wasn't calling Peter "Satan." He was addressing the same spirit that tempted Jesus in the wilderness and attempted to derail His destiny (Matthew 4:1–11). Peter was an easy target for the Enemy due to his impetuous and hasty nature.

The Enemy targets Christians every day of the week. When we operate in fear or control, or react anxiously, the Enemy is right there to leverage our circumstances against us. When we harbor bitterness or anger, the Enemy gains a foothold (Ephesians 4:27). When we disobey God, sin intentionally, gossip, betray others—the list goes on—we open the doors and windows of our souls to Satan's influence. The Enemy acts as a legalist. If we grant him legal ground to occupy our territory, he will take it.

That's why we need to deal with our fleshly tendencies; they tell us something about what we believe and who we trust. We don't need shame or condemnation to help us discern our weak spots. We need the loving, life-giving Holy Spirit to shine His light in our hearts so we see what we need and then follow His lead. The fear of the Lord is truly the beginning of wisdom.

> The fear of the Lord is the beginning of wisdom,
> And the knowledge of the Holy One is understanding.
>
> (PROVERBS 9:10 NKJV)

When your flesh surfaces and your "self-sins" start to show, don't fall into condemnation. Don't hang your head in shame. Instead, consider it information—and even an invitation. An old pastor friend used to say, "Susie, when your 'stuff' surfaces, don't despair. Be glad! That's just God reaching into your soul, pulling out what needs to go, and declaring, 'You see this? I'm about to deliver you from it!'" I love that!

The One who merely spoke and the heavens came to be, is real. He's alive and active and has things to say to you. Because Christ is in you, the most accurate understanding of who you are in Him is this:

YOU'RE BEAUTIFUL, BELOVED, BOLD, AND BRAVE.

YOU'RE LOVED, CHERISHED, AND CALLED TO A MIRACULOUS LIFE.

YOU CARRY THE TREASURE OF THE LIVING GOD WITHIN YOU.

ALL OF HEAVEN KNOWS YOUR NAME. HELL DOES TOO. BOTH SIDES HAVE AN OPINION ABOUT YOUR LIFE, BUT THEY BOTH AGREE ON YOUR WORTH.

THE ENEMY IS TERRIFIED THAT YOU'LL FINALLY DISCOVER AND BELIEVE WHO YOU REALLY ARE, BECAUSE WHEN YOU DO, YOU'LL BE UNSTOPPABLE.

YOUR PRECIOUS FATHER LOOKS AT YOU WITH KIND, LOVING EYES AND WANTS YOU TO BELIEVE WHAT HE SAYS ABOUT YOU.

KEEP AN EAR BENT TOWARD HEAVEN. LISTEN FOR HIS VOICE. YOU'RE AN ABSOLUTE TREASURE TO HIM.

Everyone's heart needs healing in some way. Are you open to transformation? Are you willing to acknowledge where your heart hurts? If the Holy Spirit woke you up at 4:00 a.m. and invited you to get out of bed and spend time with Him, would you respond? God has so much more for you than you can imagine. But it begins with a humble, receptive heart. It begins with your willingness to follow Jesus wherever He leads. God is not predictable, but He is purposeful.

You can trust Him.

Dr. Saundra Dalton-Smith writes: "Healing requires your participation, your yielded yes. Yes to the process. Yes to the messiness. Yes to the stretching. Yes to the unknown. Yes to help. Yes to support. Yes to beholding God's intervention. The healing begins with your yes. As you yield your need to understand and have all the answers, you open the door for God to enter the situation."[4]

Following Jesus isn't easy; it costs us everything, but we gain even more. We gain heaven, wholeness, everlasting joy, healing, redemption, unending fellowship with loved ones, and eternal intimacy with God the Father, Jesus the Son, and the precious, powerful Holy Spirit. Imagine it! It's more than worth it. *He's* more than worth it!

As we allow Him to lead, He guides us along paths of humility, healing, and wholeness. He renews and refreshes, redeems and restores, convicts and corrects—all with a heart of steadfast love. We're on a pilgrimage to the Holy City, and He will get us there safely. But we have work to do in the meantime and a passionate, loving God to reflect accurately. We don't want His love to get lost in translation.

If we don't believe it for ourselves, how can we ever convince others? Can we impart what we don't possess?

Even so, we get to be a work in progress without the condemnation. We get to take our messy, unhealed, hopeful selves and follow Jesus with our whole hearts. And what does He do? He works wonders in and through us! He ministers life to us! He reveals His nature to us. He makes a way for us. There's no better place to be—in any season of life—than walking in intimacy with our Savior.

> The more we grasp who Jesus is, the more we comprehend all we were created to be.

As we put our hope in Him, we will be changed. The degree to which we learn to submit to His rule and reign will determine to what degree we walk in His power, purpose, and authority. The more we grasp who Jesus is, the more we comprehend all we were created to be.

PRAYER

Father in heaven,

Holy is Your name. May Your kingdom come, and may Your will be done on earth, in me, and in our day! Awaken me to the reality of Your great love for me. Ignite fresh faith within me! Open my eyes to see You in ways I have never seen before.

Heighten my sensitivity to Your precious Holy Spirit alive in me. Grant me a deeper love for Your Word and an increased capacity to understand it. Heal and transform me into someone I never dreamed I could be! I believe in Your miracle-working power!

I am Yours, and You are mine. Your banner over me is love.
I'm waiting, watching, learning, and changing because of Your transformative work in my life.
My soul waits for You!
Amen.

MOMENTS OF REFLECTION

1. Read Matthew 16:13–27 and reflect on a time when God revealed something about His nature or character to you. And if that's never happened for you, spend some time reading Psalm 103 to get a vision for what God is like. Ask Him to speak to your heart. What does Psalm 103 tell us about God? Write down your thoughts.

2. What do you love most about Jesus?

3. Prayerfully ask God this question: *Lord, who do You say that I am?* Write down what He shows you.

Chapter Three

GOD FILLS ME WITH UNWAVERING FAITH

If we go to God in everything, we'll have wisdom and discernment on every needed occasion—which is just about always. . . . He is a friend closer than a brother, richer than a trillionaire, wiser than a scholar, greater than a ruler.

ROBERT J. MORGAN,
WHATEVER HAPPENS

Let us seize and hold tightly the confession of our hope without wavering, for He who promised is reliable and trustworthy and faithful [to His word].

HEBREWS 10:23 AMP

If someone asked you about the most significant, transformative part of your story, what might you tell them? Would you talk about that season when the wind was at your back, and everything fell into place? Or would you take them to that moment when you army crawled through your valley and found the strength to trust God for your next steps? Most people refer to their trials when they talk about the crucial parts of their story. That's the part we want to hear from each other because it means we're not alone. Your resilience shows others it's possible to survive what feels impossible.

Our battles shape us (if we frame them and fight them rightly). My grandma used to say, "Your trials will either make you better or bitter. You decide." I'd even say that our trials keep us out of trouble. But I'll write more about that later.

They say that we're either walking into a storm, through a storm, or out of a storm. Wherever life finds you today, what do you need from the Lord? Strength? Wisdom? More wind in your sails? Perspective amid the chaos? Whatever it is, God has what you need, and you lay hold of it by laying hold of Him. He is life and He is here for you.

You know what He wants from you? He wants your trust. He loves your faith. And He wants to teach you new things as you journey together on the path He has for you. Whatever He allows, He redeems. So whatever you're walking through in this very moment is packed with eternal and redemptive possibilities.

My friend is in the fight of her life. I'll call her Marie. From the outside looking in, she displays the picture of health and a wealth of faith. Very few know of her private struggle, and she wants it that way.

A couple of years ago, she started to experience scary neurological symptoms. As a nurse, she's versed in symptoms that likely point to devastating diagnoses. At first, she panicked, as anyone would. But it didn't take her long to get her game on. She armored up, pressed into God like never before, and refused to succumb to the disease that threatened her. Before this battle, she was already a serious Christ follower. Intensely purposeful in how she walks with God. Excellent in her field of health care. And a fierce athletic competitor.

The devil picked the wrong girl to mess with. I've never seen anything like it and never known anyone like her. It's been two years of debilitating symptoms, yet Marie grows spiritually stronger each day. In addition to her regular prayer time, she has added what she calls her "hour of power." Marie spends an hour each day on her knees, reciting Scripture, worshiping God, and reminding her soul of how faithful God is to His Word.

God continues to give her vivid dreams of overcoming and ministering healing to those who lack the fight she possesses. She fasts twice weekly and presses in with renewed fervency on those days. Marie also created a battle box—a plastic container filled with her go-to Scriptures that have kept her in the fight. Every day, she opens her battle box and prays the promises of God over her life. She says, "Rehearsing God's promises out loud obliterates all fear within me." She has fully surrendered her life to the process and timing of God. The girl is on fire! Thanks to Marie, I now have my own battle box.

GOD TREASURES YOUR FAITH

Let me say a word to those who have battled and contended for *years*. I know this struggle well. I've fought for full healing from the effects of

Lyme disease for over three decades. These symptoms have knocked me down and taken me out too many times to count. I'll tell you more about these battles in the chapters to come. But I will say that I always come up swinging. I feel better when there is faith in my heart. I do better when there is purpose in my steps. If you have been battling for a long time, I wish I could wrap you in a hug and whisper a prayer for you. In fact, I've had the privilege of embracing and praying for countless women across the country. I long to see a wave of healing sweep through our land, especially for those who have fought long and hard for their freedom and wholeness.

I know God's ways are a mystery. I don't understand why some receive miraculous healing on this side of heaven while others do not. I refuse to believe it's because they missed a step or lacked sufficient faith. God gifts us with faith. Yes, we must steward it, but He is far more gracious with us than we are with ourselves. In fact, when you read through the "Hall of Faith," as recorded in Hebrews 11, you find that some people died without receiving what God had promised them.

As a young believer, I often wondered, *Then what's the point of faith in His promises?* But as I grew, I learned that life on earth is short, and eternity is forever. If we don't receive the promise in this life, it's because the answer is too glorious for earth to contain. And those heroes in the Hall of Faith who died before receiving the promise? Scripture says that "the world was not worthy of them" (Hebrews 11:38 NIV). I know many godly believers who stood strong in faith until the very end. You'll never convince me that they missed a step. I tend to believe that the world was not worthy of them.

You must discern for yourself what kind of faith God has imparted to you. Is it a fledgling faith? A mountain-moving faith? You know, a mustard-seed-sized faith is all you need. Wherever you are today, remember that faith doesn't grow without active, persistent use.

If you are in Christ, *Christ is in you*, which means He has imparted a measure of faith to you. Have you activated that gift of faith recently? Are you contending for a breakthrough? Believing God for mountains to move? Are you responding to the promises of God? If you're confused about the idea of faith, just ask God to show you what He's given you faith for, what promises He wants you to stand on, and how to apply that faith practically to your current situation.

God has given you a gift of faith, but you're the one who gets to steward His promises in a way that fits your particular season of life. So, dare to ask yourself, *Am I settling for less than God's best for me?* Since your faith pleases God and is more precious to Him than gold, trust Him to train you to walk in faith. It's like exercising a muscle. It's learning to trust more in His promises than in what your eyes see. Faith isn't a feeling. It's not an emotion. It's "the substance of things hoped for, the evidence of things" yet unseen (Hebrews 11:1 NKJV).

I've noticed that when I quiet the external noise and immerse myself in God's Word and worship for extended periods, I rise from that place with a deep and strong sense of my God-given authority. Because I walk in step with the Spirit, I speak with precision and pray with power. We're the *best* version of ourselves when we walk in the Spirit!

Because I walk in step with the Spirit, I speak with precision and pray with power. We're the *best* version of ourselves when we walk in the Spirit!

Just look at the stories from Scripture. When someone called by God reacts in fear or self-preservation, they make a mess of things. But when that same person dares to trust God's Word and do what He says, we see miracles happen.

When I walk intimately with God and rely deeply on His input, I suddenly remember verses I memorized years ago. I recall stories from Scripture that I haven't read in ages. I share wisdom and insights that are as new to me as they are to the person I'm talking to. Scripture reminds us that God confides in those who fear Him (Psalm 25:14; Jeremiah 33:3; John 14:26). He tells us things we wouldn't otherwise know. And He brings to remembrance things He's spoken to us in the past. When I walk in the Spirit, I have peace, perspective, and a strong sense that God is with me.

> When I walk in the Spirit, I have peace, perspective, and a strong sense that God is with me.

Conversely, when I squander time on social media or cable news, I feel my self-life starting to show. For example, I'm quickly discouraged, easily distracted. And I lack the power in my steps that I know God has made available to me. It's never worth it to appease the lazy side of me. Just sayin'.

Activated faith keeps me dependent on God, empowers my prayers, and changes me from the inside out.

So what about you? How have your battles strengthened you? Your battles for healing and against fear? Your battles for family or for your purpose? Have you, at times, given in too quickly when the Enemy sought to torment, taunt, or steal from you? What might a fiercer faith look like in you and on you?

Even now, you're facing battles and challenges that could serve you well in the days ahead. May God show you the promises that are yours for the taking in this season. Build your own battle box, armor up, and reclaim the territory God has promised you! God not only treasures you for who you are, but He also sees you for who you can become. Every blessing, every battle in your life is an invitation to engage with God so He can transform you and redeem your story.

DISCERNING THE DIFFERENCE BETWEEN DISCIPLINE AND HYPERVIGILANCE

When you've walked the long road of suffering and are waiting for a breakthrough, it's easy to surrender to your circumstances and allow them to define you, or take matters into your own hands without seeking God's help and intervention.

God has wired me to be a disciplined person. But when it seemed He was taking too long to heal me and bring the breakthrough I so desperately longed for, I took discipline to a whole new level. One of the reasons I became so hypervigilant is that my body reacted so strongly to the slightest issues. It was maddening. While other healthy people could eat whatever they wanted, go to bed whenever they wanted, and exercise at whatever intensity they wanted, I was left with a hypersensitive system. I pay a price if I am careless with my disciplines. It's not in my head. It's my reality. Maybe you can relate.

I remember several years ago, during one of my intense battles with scary, runaway symptoms, I paced the floor at night, crying out to God, quoting Scripture, and waiting for Him to speak to me. He thundered something in my spirit that I'll never forget. He said, *Susie, you acquire a healthy life by stewardship, but you acquire a healed life by faith.*

God is not obligated to keep us healthy if we keep making self-destructive choices. What we sow is what we grow. But the kind of true healing that we all need (heart, mind, body, soul) does not come from striving, perfecting our disciplines, and doing it right all the time. It comes from the Spirit of the living God, who is mightily at work within us as we trust Him in increasing measure.

I pray regularly, *Lord, align my heart with Yours! Align my will with*

Yours! May I lose my appetite for that which weakens me. Give me a hunger for all that's right and good and for that which pleases You. Spirit of the living God, heighten my sensitivity to Your influence in my life. Help me respond to the slightest wisp of the Spirit within me. Give me a hunger and a thirst for Your highest and best will for me!

Though God's grace is abundant and He's good to us every single day, it doesn't mean that He's "good" with everything we do. Our choices matter. Our choices have consequences. Relying on God's goodness is one thing. Presuming upon His goodness is another.

As children of God, we live to please Him. We care about what He cares about. And we deal with the sinful tendencies within us that pull us from His best for us.

> Don't be misled—you cannot mock the justice of God. You will always harvest what you plant. Those who live only to satisfy their own sinful nature will harvest decay and death from that sinful nature. But those who live to please the Spirit will harvest everlasting life from the Spirit. (Galatians 6:7–8)

If faith is trusting and letting go of control, what exactly should we try to exert influence over in this life? How do we strike the balance between taking action and letting go? God certainly calls us to take action. Discipline in life is essential. Purposely pursuing God makes a difference in your life. In fact, He rewards those who earnestly seek after Him (Hebrews 11:6)!

Self-control is one of the fruits of the Spirit. Scripture tells us that a life without control "is like a city with broken-down walls" (Proverbs 25:28). Historically, kings often inspected the city wall for low, broken-down places when wars ceased. Those were the very places they were vulnerable to enemy attack. It's the same with you and me. The areas in our lives where we indulge without restraint, are not open to correction, or are hyperfocused on controlling outcomes, are the areas the Enemy has his eye on. He's watching for the right moment to steal, kill, and destroy (John 10:10).

Yes, there's a place in our lives for discipline and self-control. We need to work that muscle regularly. Just because you can eat, buy, drink, or do something doesn't mean you should. This is not for legalism's sake but for wisdom's sake.

That said, when we walk through prolonged, terrifying battles, we can overdevelop our disciplines to the point of hypervigilance, which is not sourced from the Vine. Spirit-led restraint is God-given empowerment. Fierce faith is Spirit-given and Spirit-sustained. Hypervigilance is based on fear and control. There's no grace in hypervigilance. It's all on you, and you'd better do it right. It's impossible to be in faith and hypervigilance at the same time.

For example, when it seemed that God was silent regarding my health battles with Lyme, I took matters into my own hands. I extensively researched healthy supplements and detox protocols (nothing wrong with that, right?). But then I took it to an extreme; if I missed a dose, ran out of a supplement, or treated myself to a gluten-free, dairy-free sweet treat, I'd feel guilty (because sugar causes inflammation, and I couldn't afford more inflammation), which then morphed into fear. I offered myself no grace. I was captive to my own laws and in bondage to my striving-for-perfection-but-imperfect performance. Discipline helped me get healthy. Hypervigilance put me in bondage.

> It's impossible to be in faith and hypervigilance at the same time.

Our faith compels us to fix our eyes on Jesus, who is always doing something new in us (Hebrews 12:2). Faith surrenders control and outcomes to the One who knows best while holding fast to holy expectancy. Faith knows God is on it, and He's up to something good! Sometimes, faith hangs on, grabs the promise, and stands firm. But sometimes, faith looks like letting go, resting for a while, and experiencing God on a deeper level.

Contending for God's promises is not about fighting harder to get relief from stress. It's about paying attention to what God allows to surface within you and discerning your best strategy with Him. One way you know you're on the right track is when God's strategy for you defies your flesh's most comfortable inclination.

Left to myself, I default to self-protection, so when God's strategy involves me stepping out, taking some risks, or facing my fears, I know it's time for deeper dependence on God and a more engaged faith. Left to myself, I could be a monk because I thrive on solitude and reflection. So when God's answer to my prayers involves calling me into a crowd, or to an unknown city, or to a party where there's mostly small talk, I know it's time to die to my love of comfort and quietness, and live for Christ, wherever He leads me. If I really want God's input in my life, I must know that when I ask for more from Him, He'll ask for more from me.

How about you? It may require faith for you to quit that extra job. So, what's the promise you should hold on to? It's this: My God will supply all my needs according to His riches in glory (Philippians 4:19)!

Or perhaps you're trying to control a relationship that is beyond your control. Or you're longing for your prodigal to come home, or your marriage to be revived, or your body to be healed. There's a promise in Scripture for you that will require faith to embrace. The kind of faith that contends for the promises knows when to let go and rest and when to rise with a holy roar. Search the Scriptures and find God's living, breathing promise to you.

It's important to note that we often get ahead of ourselves when we choose our promise before hearing from the Lord. Where the flesh is allowed to thrive, where striving, control, and hypervigilance prevail, there will be no power, deliverance, or breakthrough. We reinforce our own captivity when we take control of our circumstances. But "where the Spirit of the Lord is, there is freedom" (2 Corinthians 3:17 NIV).

Where in your story is God inviting you to active, engaged faith?

Wait. Before you answer that question, just pause for a moment and consider this: The God of the universe invites you to engage with Him on a deeper level! There's no hardship He can't redeem. No mountain He can't move. But He allows our battles to make us warriors who are no longer bullied by our fears or intimidated by our obstacles.

Faith isn't for the prideful or the cowardly. It requires humility to admit you're dependent and grit to hang in there when your love of comfort and convenience is begging for control. But there's no way we'll ever know what we're capable of, and what God is willing to do, unless *faith* is central to our story.

Dr. Sharon Hodde Miller writes: "Even if our motives are just slightly off, just slightly selfward, and we attach God's name to them, we can distort someone's entire perception of God. This is what made Jesus's life and teaching so remarkable. Jesus's use of spiritual power did not distort but clarified who God is and what he is like."[1]

FILL YOUR JARS

When all seems hopeless, what does it look like to believe for a miracle in faith? In the book of 2 Kings, we read how this played out in the story of the prophet Elisha.[2]

One day, the widow of a prophet came to Elisha and cried out,

PAUSE.

BREATHE.

PONDER.

There's a fine line between active faith and selfish striving.

There's also a fine line between resting and settling.

Are you settling or striving?

What are you believing God for right now?

What's He asking of you?

"My husband who served you is dead, and you know how he feared the Lord. But now a creditor has come, threatening to take my two sons as slaves."

Elisha listened intently, opened his hands, and asked, "What can I do to help you? Tell me, what do you have in the house?" The woman's shoulders dropped, along with her gaze. She replied, "I have nothing at all. Nothing, except a flask of oil."

Unwavering and with full confidence, Elisha's energy surged. He stretched out his arm, pointed to her neighbors' homes, and said, "Go! Borrow as many empty jars as you can from your friends and neighbors. Then go into your house with your sons and shut the door behind you. Pour olive oil from your flask into the jars, setting each one aside when it's filled."

The woman at once turned and did exactly as Elisha had instructed. Her two sons hurried around the neighborhood, gathering jars and bringing them to their mother. She filled one jar after another until each one was full. Soon, every jar was filled to the brim!

Excitedly, she turned to one of her sons and shouted, "Bring me another jar!" He replied, "There aren't any more, Ima. That's all of them." Once every jar was filled, the olive oil stopped flowing. She ran out to Elisha and told him what had happened. He smiled kindly and said, "Now sell the olive oil and pay your debts, and you and your sons can live on what is left over."

There's something about activated, feisty faith that so inspires me! This dear woman had watched her husband steward his calling in the fear of the Lord. I'm sure part of their ministry was caring for those in need, because anyone who sincerely walks with God also cares for the needs around them. If this prophet was anything like Elisha, he listened to the Lord, walked in His way, and helped people along the way.

Imagine the loss for this dear woman! Her God-fearing husband had passed into eternity and was no longer there to guard and guide her. Women in ancient culture were especially vulnerable without their men. If a woman lost her husband, she needed her sons. Imagine being a grieving widow who is facing the loss (and enslavement) of her two sons. Hebraic law allowed people to pay their debts by selling themselves or their children. But they were not to be treated as slaves. It sounds like this creditor's threats defied the spirit of the law.

Did she just lie down and allow this misfortune and injustice? Absolutely not! She remembered her history with God! First, she went to God's prophet and did what he told her to do. Then she called her friends and asked them to offer their jars in her time of need.

There are certain benefits in walking with God and trusting in His name. We all want miracles, but who wants to experience the kinds of crises that call for them? We like to be self-sufficient, but we are not meant to attempt this journey alone, without our people. So what can we learn from her on our journey toward discovering our most redeemed selves through faith in desperate times? Let's break down this story a bit.

First, *the woman refused to settle in her day of crisis*. She believed there was an answer for her. Far too many Christians settle in times of crisis. They either fight in the flesh or don't fight at all. Certain privileges come with being a child of God. A perfect, suffering-free life is not one of them. But in our sorrow, in our hardship, we have an Advocate. We have a Defender. We have a Provider. We have access to the presence of the living God. Scripture tells us that His faithful promises are our armor and protection (Psalm 91:4). We're *never* without help in our times of trouble.

Even if you look at your situation and see no way out, know this: There's always a way out, or through, or around. God makes a way where there is no way. He's the Waymaker. Involve God in your process and you'll see God intervene in a way that only He can.

Second, this dear woman *refused to believe that her life would be marked by only loss and no miracles.* Yes, her crisis was serious, but God ensured she had something to work with. Elisha asked her what she had, and what she had was a little oil. God multiplied the oil. In this story, we're dealing with literal oil, but in the Scriptures, oil often represents the presence and power of the Holy Spirit and the endorsement of almighty God.

But what else? Third, *she didn't do it alone* (2 Kings 4:3). In this time of crisis, Elisha encouraged her not to isolate but to include her friends in the miracle. She needed their jars—their expectancy that something was about to happen. God would fill the jars she gathered, and God will fill our hearts beyond our level of expectancy. Whatever you need in your crisis, you have in abundance in God, your Father.

But here's an important point to remember: God gives us help, yes, and you can borrow someone's faith in the short run (friends' faith can carry us through the most difficult times). But to run *your* race, you need your own thriving, growing, activated faith.

God will use circumstances, miracles, community, His Word, and the power of His Spirit to activate our faith. We grow and heal in community, but our faith must be our own. Our faith is formed by our daily choice to believe what God says when our circumstances tell another story.

God will fill our hearts beyond our level of expectancy. Whatever you need in your crisis, you have in abundance in God, your Father.

Remember my friend Marie, who fought for her faith during her struggles with neurological symptoms? And the battle box she made, full of verses she could pull out to strengthen her faith and her prayers? She's an absolute powerhouse of faith, and it started to catch on with those around her.

One day, her sister asked her to come and pray for her husband, who battled a brain tumor. Marie armored up and went over to their house to pray. She spoke with such authority and knew God's Word so profoundly that they both were overwhelmed by God's presence when she prayed.

The following morning, Marie's sister told her husband, "I'm going to pay Marie to make me a battle box, write down every verse she has memorized and rehearsed, and document everything she learned from this battle. I want to pray with that kind of authority!" Her husband wisely replied, "You can't buy her oil. It's not for sale. You have to pay for your own oil."

His insight reminds me of something Dr. Rob Reimer often says on my radio show: "You can have as much of God as you want. But not more than you're willing to pay the price for." New battles often require new strategies. Often when facing giants or mountains, we need to up our game and engage with God on a deeper level. Is God asking you to commit to fasting one day a week? Or to memorize more Scriptures? Or to create a battle box of your own?

Maybe He's asking you to connect with your most fiery prayer warrior friends and pray over the phone once a week. Or to dedicate an hour a week soaking in worship music as you rest in Him. God knows what you need and He'll inspire your choices.

When our spiritual disciplines become rote and second nature, it's time for some cross-training. I've paid a heavy price for some of the battles I've walked through. I've memorized a lot of Scripture as I've walked the floor in the middle of the night praying out loud.

I've trimmed the fat off my life during battle and pressed in with more fervency than I ever had before. Yet, let me tell you something: What I've found in God, what I've experienced in His nearness in the middle of my storms, has been priceless. If not for my storms, I never would have experienced Him as my shelter and my covering and my safe place. He's worth any price we pay to lay hold of more of Him.

My friend Marie says we coddle ourselves too much and cave too quickly when the battle rushes in. I thought I was intense in prayer, but Marie has fueled my flame! And would you believe she continues to win platinum medals? None of her opponents or coaches know about the physical symptoms that continue to surface and affect how she functions.

This is not to say it's been easy. It's been a brutal battle. But I'm watching a miracle unfold before my eyes. I believe God is going to use her to bring healing to the multitudes who deal with devastating neurological diseases for which there are no cures. Her fight and her faith have fueled mine.

One day, I texted Marie and asked how she was doing. Here's her text response to me:

> The battle has been a challenge, but I'm focusing on what I can do and not on what is difficult. It's hard! I have to keep my head in the game, trust in the journey and that I'm on God's pathway forward. I have been listening to many sermons about faith versus believing and hearing how faith is built in opposition, battles, and wilderness seasons. You can "believe" without opposition, but NOT SO with faith. Faith is developed in the struggle and in fierce opposition! God moves on faith, and we can only develop faith in the battle.

> Lots of opposition = lots of faith building = lots of hard-earned faith = great and mighty moves of God. God moves on our developed faith! Thinking about that strengthens me. There is a higher purpose in this struggle. We need to develop a lot of faith for the work God has for us to do in the future.

And that's just it, isn't it? Nobody wants the kind of opposition that leads to faith building. Not at first. Nobody wants to find themselves in those scary moments when the future seems uncertain. Where you are desperate and down to your last jar of oil. But if you can remember during those times that you have complete access to God, His power, and His promises, you will discover God to be immensely faithful. You'll also realize that God always seeks to deepen and even enhance your sense of identity, using your most challenging moments to impress these truths on your heart.

You have some decisions to make, and it's best you make them before the storm hits. Will you, like the widow in 2 Kings, refuse to settle in the day of crisis? Will you choose to believe right here and now that God is still a miracle-working God? Will you allow others into the vulnerable parts of your story, maybe borrow their faith if necessary, and watch God provide? Are you ready to make your faith your own? To work your faith muscle in a way that pleases God and changes your story? No pressure here, but know that others are watching if and how you develop your faith.

Chip Ingram joined me on my show recently. He said the best thing: "God is so good, kind, and gentle that whatever you're going through right now, know that as hard as it is, this is God's kindest, gentlest way to bring about the change and transformation in your life that could be accomplished no other way. If there were any other way for Him to accomplish His best purposes in you and for you, He would. There's grace for you in this struggle, and He will see you through."[3]

God *intends* to bless you. He sings over you. His plans and intentions toward you are far better than anything you can imagine. And God can redeem whatever people or circumstances have stolen from you many times. He can and will redeem your mistakes. He works all things—not just some things but *all things*—together for your good and His glory (Romans 8:28).

May God give you a fresh vision of who you're becoming because you trust Him. May He impart fresh faith for the journey ahead. May you dare to imagine a more healed, strengthened, bold, courageous you. Picture it! Imagine others being strengthened by the firepower in your soul. Your most redeemed self is a precious gift to the world. Life gets so much better when we trust Him.

PRAYER

Father in heaven,

Mighty is Your name! Holy are Your ways! I bow in reverence before You with open hands and say, "There is no one like You, Lord!"

I refuse to take a passive role in my story! But I also refuse to insert myself where You're already working. I will rest in You and hold fast to Your promises.

Show me the difference between striving from a scarcity mindset and contending, because I know what You've promised me. My soul waits for You, Lord. Show me the path of life. Remind me who I am because of who You are.

In Jesus's name I pray, amen.

MOMENTS OF REFLECTION

1. Read 2 Kings 4:1–7 and ask the Lord to speak to you about your level of expectancy. Does it correlate with your level of need?

2. God wants you to involve certain people in your story. He wants you to be honest with them and dare to ask for their help, prayers, and input. Who are those people for you?

3. How is God forging your faith in this season of life?

Chapter Four

GOD CULTIVATES GOOD FRUIT IN ME

Your troubles aren't the end of your story. You're a kintsugi vessel whose fractures are mended by the gold of God's grace. Your real story is in the golden seams.

ALAN WRIGHT, *THE POWER TO BLESS*

If you remain in Me and My words remain in you [that is, if we are vitally united and My message lives in your heart], ask whatever you wish and it will be done for you. My Father is glorified and honored by this, when you bear much fruit, and prove yourselves to be My [true] disciples.

JOHN 15:7–8 AMP

One of the things I love about Jesus is that He never acted like a celebrity or a VIP. The Son of God laid down His life. He served the least and the lowest. He was content to be misunderstood for the greater good. He was not too big for small things. And never too small for big things.

He washed feet, healed the sick, restored the brokenhearted, and multiplied loaves and fishes. He confronted bullies, comforted outcasts, and saved humankind. I love Jesus. I love how He lived. I love that He lived. I'm perpetually in awe that He died and then blew the doors off the devil's claim on you and me. I marvel that, at this moment, He's interceding for us both. I wonder what He's praying for you right now.

Jesus's life was antithetical to the celebrity culture of our day.

And that's why I wanted to stop speaking at women's events.

Let me explain.

While God has accomplished so much in me through my battle with Lyme disease (along with chronic neurological symptoms as a result), it hasn't exactly been a walk in the park. Ten years ago, I experienced a significant health relapse that felt like a journey through hell. Apparently, individuals with chronic Lyme issues also struggle with processing mold. I had been unknowingly and repeatedly exposed to black mold while navigating some excruciating life circumstances that broke our hearts. The combination created a perfect storm.

The mold affected my brain and cognitive function in a way that terrified me. I work every day doing live radio. Suddenly, my face, tongue, and neck would go numb, and I couldn't remember the words I needed for my sentences. I was writing my umpteenth book but suddenly couldn't recall how to spell basic words. Surges of inflammation coursed through my body at the most unexpected times. I experienced stroke-like symptoms in the middle of the night, and my heart would beat wildly in my chest. I'd walk the floor all night quoting Scripture, praying, and deep breathing. By morning, I was exhausted.

On numerous occasions, I cried out to God, "Lord, You're going to have to either take me or heal me. I don't have the mental bandwidth to navigate this storm."

When you travel across the country and speak at churches and conferences, you take a significant risk of staying in mold-infested buildings. Mold is everywhere, even in nice, newer-looking structures (if they weren't properly constructed). It pained me to include the clause in my contract, "Marriott or better." I feared being misunderstood and being lumped with those who demand accommodations because they think they are important. I didn't want to be remotely associated with that kind of celebrity culture.

But each time I took the risk of staying in an older hotel, the pressure in my head returned, along with the debilitating symptoms. If mold only caused my body to ache, I wouldn't mind. But I need my brain to function, and it's dangerous for me to continuously expose myself to buildings that make me sick.

Although I have made great progress, mold still affects me. I feel embarrassed to ask for accommodations that have low risk of mold, and I need to recover each time I stay in moldy camps, churches, or hotels. Sometimes it takes me weeks to recover.

One day, as Kev and I checked into our room for a speaking event, I whispered to him (even though we were the only ones present), "I'm going to stop speaking after these next few events. I can't keep asking people to accommodate me; it's embarrassing. Maybe this isn't the right thing for me." In his wisdom, Kev simply smiled and squeezed my shoulder.

The next day, after my first session, I stood behind my book table and looked at the long line of women waiting to speak with me. I love praying one-on-one with women, so these moments are always precious to me.

Suddenly, I spotted a beautiful Black woman in vibrant clothing moving from the back of the line. She wore orange-red pants and a silk blouse that featured hues of gold, purple, yellow, and that same orange-red shade. A silk scarf draped over her shoulder, which she kept whipping back. She swayed her hips with confidence and told the women as she passed, "I'm not buttin'. I'm just sayin'. I'm not buttin'. I'm just sayin'." She had a feistiness about her that instantly drew me to her. *We could be friends*, I thought.

It felt as though everyone else faded to the background. All I could see was this beautiful, vibrant woman making her way to the front of the line. When she finally reached me, she rested her hands on the book table, leaned in close to my face, pointed at me, and said, "Susie Larson. You listen to me. Don't even think about quitting or turning back from the call of God on your life! God is the One who called you. He's the One who will sustain you. Don't you dare think about quitting!"

I stood there, stunned. No words. I watched her walk away, then looked up at Kev as if to ask what just happened. He chuckled, threw his hands in the air in innocence, and said, "I didn't say anything!" Then he smiled again, but this time with a little spark in his eyes. After the session, I searched for the woman and asked others if they had seen her. Nobody had. But how could you miss her? As Kev and I walked out of the conference center, he leaned in and said, "Leave it to

God to give you a sassy, bossy angel to tell you what's what." I laughed out loud, but her words had pierced me too.

What was I afraid of? What was I trying to protect myself from?

- Being misjudged?
- Being lumped together with "celebrity Christians"?
- Getting sick again?

Was God aware of my struggle? Yes, He was. Did He understand my fears? Absolutely. Did He care that some might misjudge me? He cared but wasn't too worried about it because people misjudged Him all the time. They still do.

Is God big enough to handle my issues?

More than big enough.

Is my identity up for grabs just because I need a few accommodations? Not in the least. I am a child of God, filled with the Spirit of the living God, and empowered by Him alone. I have authority in Christ on my weak days and my strong days. On my messy days and my better-looking days. So do you.

I shudder to think what might have happened if I had quit early just to feel more comfortable. Something changed in me after my encounter with that beautiful angel of a woman. I set my face like flint and knew I would triumph (Isaiah 50:7). Since then, we've experienced an upsurge in breakthroughs and even healings at our events. I've developed greater resilience to push through in less-than-ideal conditions. We see more fruit and favor in our obedience to God, especially when it's risky or feels outside our comfort zone.

The Enemy of your soul would love for you to self-sabotage. Preempt an outcome because you're afraid or uncomfortable. You will face opposition, delays, and detours when you trust God and follow His lead.

Don't be dismayed by the obstacles; ask God to show you your strategy. Setbacks are only temporary for those who serve in God's kingdom.

Just because something is hard doesn't mean God's not in it. Anything that draws us into a deeper dependence on God *is a blessing*. Fruit comes from the abiding life (not from ideal circumstances that promise comfort and convenience). Favor surrounds us because God is good and because we dare to trust Him more than we trust ourselves or our circumstances.

Don't be dismayed by the obstacles; ask God to show you your strategy. Setbacks are only temporary for those who serve in God's kingdom.

After that day, something emerged within me: a new resilience and even vitality in my calling, along with a fresh expectancy. God is mighty to save, and His strength is perfected in our weakness. I refuse to be bullied by the threats of being misunderstood. I am a child of God. He knows my weaknesses. He knows what He's doing with my life. I needed a fresh, faith-filled perspective, and God gave me one in the most unsuspecting way!

THE PERSPECTIVE YOU CHOOSE AFFECTS THE FRUIT IN YOUR LIFE

If you and I consistently frame our situations negatively, we will continue to face discouragement, despair, and doubt. If we choose to view our lives through a negative lens, we—by our own decisions—will foster unbelief, misplaced blame, and even rebellion at times. We will restrict ourselves and deny ourselves the best of what God has intended for us.

We often contribute to our struggle to believe without even realizing it. When we allow our limitations and discomforts to take center stage, we assess things incorrectly and preempt outcomes that block God's best for us.

No one can do this for you. You're the one who stewards your perspective. You're the one who chooses the story you tell yourself. But know this: How you frame your heartbreaks and hardships echoes into eternity and impacts heaven and hell. A redeemed perspective is the gateway to a miraculous life. We're made for more!

How you frame your heartbreaks and hardships echoes into eternity and impacts heaven and hell. A redeemed perspective is the gateway to a miraculous life.

Please understand that I am not challenging you to leap into the ditch of denial or embrace toxic positivity. Neither of those mindsets is beneficial for you or for those around you. God invites us to a supernatural perspective rooted in His promises and based on His character.

> I bow before your holy Temple as I worship.
> I praise your name for your unfailing love and
> faithfulness;
> for your promises are backed
> by all the honor of your name.
>
> (PSALM 138:2)

If you're walking through a challenging time, determine not to make permanent decisions because of a temporary situation. Ask God, *What does obedience look like here? How can I better trust You here? Where can I bear the most fruit in this season?* Dare to believe that right in the midst of the struggle are opportunities to flourish and find favor.

As people filled with the Spirit of the living God, we're far more spiritual than physical. As Paul put it, we carry this treasure of God in these earthen vessels, *so we'll know* that the power that marks our lives is of *God* and not of us (2 Corinthians 4:7). The Father invites us: *Look up. Trust Me. I'm closer than you know, kinder than you can imagine, and more intimately involved with your story than you can fathom. Look up, My child. I want you to see what I see.*

Do you see yourself from an eternal perspective? How about your circumstances? Are you feeling earthbound by them today? Is your narrative weakening you? Are you disappointed because you don't see the fruit you expect in your life, so you lose sight of the beautiful things God might be growing in and through you?

Perhaps it's time for a new point of view. How often do we challenge our own thought processes? When we think a thought that puts a pit in our guts or sadness in our hearts, do we stop and filter those thoughts through the lens of Scripture? Do we challenge thought processes that discourage us? Even in sad and difficult seasons, Jesus speaks to us redemptively. Our hearts can't live without hope. And we're made for peace.

Do you believe what God says about you, thinks about you, and even intends for you? Every thought He has toward you is holy (Jeremiah 29:11). Imagine that. What if your most instinctive, consistent thoughts turned your eyes upward and strengthened your faith? God wants that for you.

Paul told us to regard no one with a human point of view. That includes you!

> We have stopped evaluating others from a human point of view. At one time we thought of Christ merely from a human point of view. How differently we know him now! This means that anyone who belongs to Christ has become a new person. The old life is gone; a new life has begun! (2 Corinthians 5:16–17)

THE FRUIT OF THE SPIRIT NEVER GOES OUT OF SEASON

Summer, fall, winter, spring. The seasons of nature often reflect the seasons of our souls. These seasons come and go. Many books have been written about the seasons of the soul. How you navigate a winter season differs from how you embrace the springtime of the soul. There's a time for harvest and a time for rest, a time to seek refuge under God's wing, and a time to rise up and be counted.

Yes, we experience distinct seasons of the soul, but when it comes to the fruit of the Spirit, *fruitfulness never goes out of season* (Galatians 5:22–23). Jesus calls us to bear lasting fruit and invites us to abide with Him in every season. Whether you're sheltered under His wing or battling on the front lines, in the storm of your life or with wind at your back, fruit is possible when you remain connected to Jesus.

Though love most often thrives where faith and hope abide, it doesn't need perfect conditions to sprout, even through the hardest soil. Who's to say real fruit can't grow in a place you deem hopeless, or in an area where you feel like quitting? That's often the soil for the best miracles! Imagine emerging from a battle with a deeper sense of love, joy, and peace, with a stronger awareness of who you are because of who God is.

Joy isn't reserved for springtime; it is vibrant and powerful even in the winter seasons of our lives. To me, joy is one of the most supernatural fruits of the Spirit. The Spirit's joy fuels you with strength (Nehemiah 8:10), defies your circumstances, and grounds you in the greater realities of the kingdom.

The Enemy didn't win; you did! The devil can steal, kill, and destroy your fruit if you grant him power and access. But if you remain intimately connected to the Vine, the devil can't touch your fruit, and he despises it!

> "But blessed are those who trust in the Lord
> and have made the Lord their hope and
> confidence.
> They are like trees planted along a riverbank,
> with roots that reach deep into the water.
> Such trees are not bothered by the heat
> or worried by long months of drought.
> Their leaves stay green,
> and they never stop producing fruit."
>
> (JEREMIAH 17:7–8)

The fruit of the Spirit is the fruit of abiding intimately with Jesus. His life in you is your hope of glory (Colossians 1:27). You might be in the Enemy's crosshairs, but if you are in Christ Jesus, the Holy Spirit is alive in you, and overwhelming victory belongs to you!

STAY CONNECTED

When we make life all about us, we sow weeds into our own soil. We look inward and focus on the hard parts of our story without looking to God for a fresh perspective. We compare ourselves with those who appear to have it better than us and despair, as if God is somehow holding out on us. It's not possible to be self-obsessed and Jesus-aware at the same time. We disconnect from God's best when we interpret our circumstances without acknowledging (and being profoundly grateful for) God's divine involvement in our story.

Standing here now, marveling at the fruit we've seen in recent years, I shudder to think that I was ready to walk away from a part of my God-given calling because I didn't want to be misjudged or misunderstood, and because it didn't feel right to ask for accommodation. I had some weeds to pull, yes, but those weeds came from a faulty perspective, not from a fruitful ministry that had a cost attached to it.

The more you abide with Christ and travel at the pace of grace, the more you'll believe—in the depths of your soul—that nothing and no one can stop you from bearing fruit in every season. *You* decide if you'll cultivate such rich intimacy with God that even hell can't stop you from flourishing with nourishing fruit! God's empowering grace is available right now, in *this* moment. You can rise above a low perspective and see things as God sees them. Ask Him to help you. He will.

Your ability (and willingness) to press in for a redeemed perspective directly affects the bountiful fruit God appointed you to bear. Fruit that strengthens you and nourishes many. Even so, robust fruit develops over time, not overnight. Be patient with your process. God is.

My beautiful friend Tessa Afshar writes:

> Fruit is never produced all at once. It requires a little-by-little timeline. If you are in a little-by-little season, don't resent the slowness of your progress. Don't despise the small beginnings of God's restoration work in your soul. Open your heart to Jesus's timeline. Trust in His objective. Know that an all-at-once answer would probably

PAUSE.

BREATHE.

PONDER.

In what ways does the fear of man
keep you from trusting God?

Where in your life do you need
a redeemed perspective?

Where in your life do you
see the most fruit?

> open the door to greater problems that...would devour something good that Jesus has set aside for you.[1]

LEARNING FROM JOSEPH'S JOURNEY

Favor and favoritism are polar opposites. *Favor* comes from God for the greater purpose of the kingdom, while *favoritism* stems from man and creates an unjust culture where thriving becomes impossible. One brings fruit; the other brings rot.

In the Bible, Joseph's story shows this to us in living color (Genesis 37–50). It wasn't Joseph's fault that his father favored him over his brothers. But I'm sure his father's unequal affection influenced how Joseph connected with his siblings. Jacob's favoritism certainly affected their feelings toward him, and the brightly colored coat he'd given Joseph was a symbol that constantly reminded them. They hated Joseph to the core, to the point of plotting to kill him.

Then Joseph had a prophetic dream where he saw his brothers symbolically bowing down to him (37:6–7). Was Joseph being unwise and operating in the flesh when he shared his dream with his brothers? I'd say yes to both. He was immature and didn't know what he didn't know. Even so, the "crime" did not fit the punishment.

Imagine the jarring moment when Joseph arrived at the scene where his brothers were waiting for him. Before he had a chance to open his mouth and ask a few questions, they attacked him, tore off his beautiful robe, and threw him in a cistern. They heartlessly asked, "What will we gain by killing our brother?" (37:26). They decided to sell him into slavery instead. Can you picture Joseph's distraught face as the slave traders hauled him away in shackles? This was no joke.

Yet, no matter where Joseph ended up, the Lord was with him and blessed the work of his hands. Joseph may have been immature in his early years, but he had a righteous view of God. While working for Potiphar, things ran smoothly under his leadership. God even blessed Potiphar's livestock and crops. It was the favor of God. And who wouldn't want that?

When our sons were still at home, I often prayed that the favor of God would rest so heavily on them that they would bring a blessing wherever they worked. And God frequently answered that prayer!

Joseph was gifted, talented, conscientious, well-built, and even handsome (39:6). Potiphar's wife tried to pressure Joseph into sleeping with her, but he feared God and wanted to honor his boss, Potiphar. Joseph tried to stay out of her way, but one day, things escalated when she reached for Joseph and demanded that he go to bed with her. Joseph tore himself away and fled the scene. Humiliated, Potiphar's wife constructed a false accusation that landed Joseph in prison (39:7–18). This is just speculation here, but my guess is that if Potiphar had believed his wife, he would have had Joseph executed. The fact that he sent him to prison, possibly to save face, makes me think there's much more to this story. Perhaps Potiphar's wife had acted similarly with another man in the past.

The Lord was with Joseph in prison, demonstrating His faithful love and favor. The Lord even made Joseph a favorite of the prison warden. Soon, the warden appointed Joseph to oversee all the prisoners and every occurrence there. The favor resting upon Joseph greatly eased the warden's burden (39:21–23).

What if you walked in such favor with God that your life, service, and fruit made life better for everyone around you? What if you were so quick to deal with your heart when treated poorly that God couldn't help but bestow favor and fruitfulness on your life that defied every Enemy scheme against you?

There's so much to Joseph's story that we won't have the time to explore in this short chapter, but here are a few things I want to highlight:

Deep roots bring good fruit. Joseph was deeply committed to God, even amid relentless and unjust trials. Though he suffered greatly, he prospered remarkably. Joseph rose to the top in every situation and positively influenced those around him.

Fruit has a price. Joseph ran from sin yet paid the price as if he'd sinned. This is a foretaste and a glimpse of the coming Savior. Through Joseph's godly response to his suffering, many were saved from the famine. Through Jesus's unbearable suffering and resurrection, He made the way for us to be saved from eternal famine and enjoy His kingdom's riches forever. Wow!

Fruit blesses others. While in prison, Joseph noticed others who were downtrodden and even asked them why they were distressed (40:6–11). This moment always shocks me. Who *wouldn't* be distressed in prison, especially if unjustly accused? This moment in the story illustrates Joseph's attitude toward God. He wasn't self-absorbed or filled with self-pity; he carried himself as the leader God was shaping him to be. He proved faithful in his trials and cared for people along the way. That's fruit.

God brings about the fruit He's been growing. When Joseph's day of deliverance arrived, he went from the prison to the palace as if he was made for the palace (Genesis 41). Actually, he was. Our preparation is a long process. When the time was right, God revealed Joseph's character as well as the anointing on his life. People witnessed the power and the grace upon Joseph's life. After a long and challenging journey, God's plan for Joseph (and for Egypt) had finally come to fruition. If you stay the course, you'll marvel at God's attention to detail in your life. He's in the process of redeeming every aspect of your story.

Fruit grows in grief. Joseph named one of his sons Ephraim, which means "God has made me fruitful in this land of my grief" (41:52). Another translation reads, "God has made me fruitful in the land of my suffering" (NIV). He'll do the same for you. If you abide intimately with God in the difficult seasons, the fruit in your life will be unmistakable.

Seeing God's fruit requires a different perspective. Finally, Scripture gives us the full picture of God's plan for Joseph. Joseph wasn't left behind by his brothers. He was sent ahead because a famine was coming, and Joseph was God's appointed man to rescue a whole nation (Psalm 105:17). Sometimes you may feel left out or left behind. But know this: You're an esteemed member of the kingdom. And if for some reason you feel cast aside, it may very well mean that there's a need up ahead that you're appointed to address, and right now, He's preparing you for greatness.

Joseph named his first son Manasseh, which means "God has made me forget all my troubles" (Genesis 41:51). God does that, you know? He eventually eclipses the evil years with the good.

Scripture tells us that those who sow in tears will reap with shouts of joy (Psalm 126:5–6). We may weep and even gutturally sob when we plant our seed, but in due time, we will return with a harvest in our arms and joy in our hearts. This promise has been true in my life 100 percent of the time. God promises to work *every detail* of our lives together for our good and His glory because we belong to Him (Romans 8:28)!

He allows us to suffer much hardship, it's true. But He also brings enough good days to eclipse the bad. He—in His brilliant way—redeems our suffering. He makes something good—no, more than good. He makes something stunningly beautiful out of our lives and our stories when we dare to trust Him when none of it makes sense. We can bear robust, nourishing, life-giving fruit no matter the season. We can *walk in the Spirit* in every season. He transforms us as we go.

You don't need favoritism from man to flourish in your God-given purposes. What you want and need is the favor of God—and you have it when you walk uprightly before Him. You don't need ideal circumstances to bear fruit—fruit grows where the heart is most tender, the soil is most prepared, and where God's perspective is most embraced. Do not fret if you are in an uncomfortable season. Fear God, trust Him, and watch Him grow you right where you're planted. He'll move you, promote you, and empower you for your next place of promise when the time is ripe. Fruit and favor . . . you're made for these.

PRAYER

Precious Lord,

I bow to my knees, open my hands, and say, "Come, Lord Jesus! I want more of You!" Teach me to respond to Your beautiful invitation to know You in a deeper way than ever before. Fill me afresh with the wonder of Your love. Awaken my heart to see things as You do.

You are the source of life, and I need You every moment, every hour, every day. May we be so intimately connected that new fruit bursts forth from my life in a way that surprises me and blesses many.

Convict me deeply when I'm about to strike my own defense or take matters into my own hands. You get to decide how my life goes. You know me best and love me most.

My soul waits for You.

Amen.

MOMENTS OF REFLECTION

1. Read Genesis 39 and note that God was with Joseph, and others noticed God's favor upon Joseph's life. From your perspective, how did God's favor play out in Joseph's life? Give some concrete examples.

2. How have you seen God's hand of favor on your life?

3. In your life story, in which season of suffering or hardship have you seen the most fruit?

Chapter Five

GOD RESCUES AND RESTORES ME

Our close affiliation with our flaws leads us to question whether we are worthy of love. We can't comprehend how anyone could love us as we are, and yet God does. . . . He beckons us to come closer. He invites us into intimacy. He summons us to behold Him in all His glory.

DR. SAUNDRA DALTON-SMITH, *BEING FULLY KNOWN*

You spread out a table before me,
provisions in the midst of *attack from* my enemies;
You *care for all my needs*, anointing my head with *soothing, fragrant* oil,
filling my cup again and again *with Your grace.*

PSALM 23:5 THE VOICE

Do you love someone who is far from God? When you look at their story, do you get that familiar fist in your gut? Does it feel like it'll take an act of God to rescue them? Have no fear. God is always on a rescue mission. He leaves the ninety-nine for the one (Matthew 18:12). His eyes are on those who've been scattered, battered, or who've simply lost their way.

Know this, friend: Our God is passionate about the lost, the hurting, and the broken. He bears the weight of your burden heavier than you do. Let Him carry it. He's the One who knows how and when to encounter your loved one and lead them back to the path of life and redemption.

A friend I'll call Ashley grew up in a Christian home, was deeply involved in her Christian community, and enjoyed what seemed to be a charmed life. She acknowledges that life was so sweet that she never truly needed to rely on the Lord in any significant way. Although she often served at church, she seldom read her Bible. Reflecting on her past, she realizes how the absence of those two elements contributed to a weak spiritual foundation.

On the outside, she appeared to be the ideal Christian, but her roots didn't run very deep. She went to college and married young to a Christian man who pretended to be someone he wasn't. On their honeymoon, Ashley encountered a man different from the one she married. He insisted they return home early from their honeymoon.

To Ashley's surprise, one day her husband lost his temper. In a fit of rage, he raised a pile of heavy books over his head and threw them at her. Stunned and lying in a heap on the floor, Ashley's body surged with pain, fear, and sorrow. Bruises all over her body surfaced immediately and got darker over the next few days. The pain in her body reflected the devastation in her heart. How was this her life?

A few days later, Ashley faced her husband's rage for spending a few dollars at the grocery store without his approval. He grabbed her arms and shook her so fiercely that he left handprint bruises on her arms.

It didn't take Ashley long to realize she had made a massive mistake in marrying him. She soon became a prisoner in her own home. Meanwhile, her husband maintained the outward facade of a model Christian.

Ashley lived with Dr. Jekyll and Mr. Hyde for the next few years. He indulged in sins and addictions freely but controlled Ashley fiercely. He flaunted his sexual deviations, yet he dictated what she could wear and eat and every dollar she spent. He meticulously managed every aspect of her life. After two years, Ashley was ready to escape her abusive marriage when she discovered she was pregnant.

Ashley now had reason to rely on the Lord. She cried out to Him with all her might. She begged God to heal her marriage, fix it somehow, and even strengthen her. But God seemed silent. Ashley got mad at God. Where was He? She reached out to Christian leaders and asked for help, only to hear that God hates divorce and that she had to stay and figure out how to love this man.

Over time, Ashley had two children, a broken heart, and a deeply traumatized body from the physical, mental, and emotional abuse inflicted by a man who lived a double life. Finally mustering the courage to leave the marriage, she and her kids moved in with her parents. For the sake of her children, she didn't want to dishonor their father, so she refrained from sharing everything she'd endured. People were all too eager to blame her for the breakdown of their marriage.

Ashley couldn't take it anymore. She walked away from God. For three years, she worked as a model and an actress and ran with depraved people of significant financial means. She indulged and engaged in activities that numbed her pain, but that reinforced her captivity. Ashley found herself in a relationship with another abusive, controlling man who perpetrated much of the same treatment her husband had. She admits that she didn't see the red flags because she was so conditioned to being abused.

Things culminated for Ashley one day while on vacation with this man and his friends. He'd drunk too much and decided to hide Ashley's passport because she'd threatened to leave. Although Ashley's vacation destination and hotel accommodations were those of the rich and famous, her life had hit rock bottom. She'd reached her breaking point and didn't want this life anymore.

When Ashley demanded her passport, this enormous beast of a man picked her up and threw her across the room, breaking the bones in her foot.

Ashley was a single mom trapped in a foreign country, in need of medical attention, and unable to access her passport. Her life was a mess. "What am I doing here?" she asked herself. Ashley realized that apart from God, she was the one who had brought herself to this moment. She'd never dealt with her previous trauma, so she was destined to repeat it.

Ashley dropped to her knees and cried out to the God of her childhood, saying, "Lord, if You get me home to my babies, I'll spend the rest of my life living for You."

Ashley told me, "A half hour later, I met a man from my home state who asked about my story. He helped me get home and connected me with an amazing church community. He never judged me; he showed only compassion and kindness."

It seemed that God had opened a way of rescue.

HE ALWAYS MAKES A WAY

Ashley's new church community made a world of difference. They had just completed a twenty-one-day fast, and she heard all the testimonies that resulted from it. She decided to undertake a forty-day Daniel fast on her own. Ashley's mind, body, and soul detoxed as she consumed only healthy foods and immersed herself in God's presence. She developed an active prayer life, spending hours each day reading God's Word, unable to get enough of it!

Ashley reflected on how the moment she cried out to God, He was ready to draw her back to Himself. The same kind man who'd helped Ashley get home also introduced her to his mom, who happened to be a counselor, and encouraged Ashley to talk with her to begin sorting through her pain. God had heard her cry and set her on the path to healing.

Her new counselor, unaware of her story, said to Ashley, "God wants you to know that He sees you've been a Christian since you were very young, but you're still a spiritual newborn. You need time in the Word to grow your faith." A week later, at their next meeting, the counselor presented a picture of a waterfall and said, "Ashley, when people look at you, they see the beauty of the waterfall, but nobody sees the depth at its base. You're a deep, deep pool that is sourced in God!" Ashley slowly came back to life. Her counselor recognized who she was and who she could be long before Ashley had the faith to believe it herself.

Around day twenty-one of her fast, the Lord told Ashley she would one day do ministry. God continued to affirm Ashley's worth and confirm her identity in Christ. Eventually, Ashley met a godly man, married him, and had more children.

Once Ashley was safely loved and cared for by her amazing husband, her health deteriorated. It was as if her body held together until she was safe enough to fall apart. Ashley has battled chronic illness for years, but that's not what defines her or what stands out most about her. What makes Ashley an astonishing woman of God, in my view, is the force she represents in the kingdom. She knows God's Word, loves God's people, and deeply cares for those who make self-destructive choices because they don't know who they are.

When she finds someone in the ditch, her eyes well up with tears, and she wants to know, "What happened to you? What in you still needs healing?" Ashley is living a redeemed life. Hers is a miracle story. The Spirit of God is alive in her. She ministers with power and authority and knows how to stand in faith. She is a new creation. She lives loved.

The devil tried to take her out. He saw her potential long before she did, but he didn't win. In fact, despite her physical challenges, she speaks, writes, and ministers to young people daily. Most don't know her backstory because she's still not at liberty to share it publicly, but it is one of rescue and restoration.

God always gives her what she needs. He prepares a table for her in the presence of an Enemy who will *not* have the last say in her story! God keeps rescuing and redeeming her, as He does for you and me. Ashley is a living, breathing ministry miracle. She still covets prayer for healing. But while her physical challenges may slow her down, they do not diminish her impact. She's making a difference in the world! Praise God!

If you're coping in ways that numb your pain but that reinforce your captivity, cry out to God. He's right here. Closer than your next breath. He wants to rescue you. If you love someone who is on the run, making self-destructive choices, remember that God is in the business of rescuing wounded, traumatized souls. Don't give up hope. Don't stop praying. God hears and is moving even now. He'll put someone in their path (or yours) when the time is right. As the classic devotional *Streams in the Desert* says,

> You can sometimes actually snatch victory from the very jaws of defeat. *Faith* can change any situation, no matter how dark or difficult. Lifting your heart to God in a moment of genuine faith in Him can quickly alter your circumstances. God is still on His throne, and He can turn defeat into victory in a split second, if we will only trust Him.[1]

What if all you need to do is lift your heart and call out?

YOUR FAITH AND RAHAB'S FAITH

When circumstances challenge you, when the Enemy taunts and threatens you, and when your fears seize you, it's instinctive to seek refuge and cope in ways that aren't healthy or helpful. But when you call out in faith instead of numbing, remembering who God is and who you are, all of heaven takes notice. So does hell. That's why your faith is so precious to God. You're activating a spiritual force that has no rival. Your faith is the currency of heaven.

I love reading the Hall of Faith in Hebrews 11 because it reminds me how important faith is to God. He isn't looking for mindless robots who toe the company line; He loves and cherishes *your* heart. He responds to *your* reliance on the Holy Spirit. He loves *your* faith. The One whom all of nature knows and responds to knows and loves *you*. The sooner you believe and trust God for who He is, the sooner you will accept the truth about who He says you are. There's no way to walk in your truest identity without faith. The people we're still talking about today knew something about God that superseded what their circumstances were telling them. They took God at His word.

Now, back to the Hall of Faith.

Hebrews 11 mentions only two women in the Hall of Faith: Sarah

PAUSE.

BREATHE.

PONDER.

In what ways do you cope or numb your pain when you're stressed or hurting?

What if you fasted from those default comforts for a season?

What if you allowed your pain and discomfort to surface and asked God to meet you right in the middle of it?

In what ways, this far in your journey, has God been more than enough for you?

and Rahab. These two women are about as different as they come. Yet Scripture honors them. Why? Dr. Warren Wiersbe explains it this way:

There's no way to walk in your truest identity without faith.

> Sarah was a godly woman, the wife of the founder of the Hebrew race; and God used her dedicated body to bring Isaac into the world. But Rahab was an ungodly Gentile who worshipped pagan gods and sold her body for money. Humanly speaking, Sarah and Rahab had nothing in common. But from the *divine* viewpoint, Sarah and Rahab shared the most important thing in life: *They both had exercised saving faith in the true and living God.*[2]

I often wonder, What kind of trauma did Rahab endure at an early age? No young girl dreams of selling her body for profit or survival. I know there's more to this story, and I look forward to sitting down with Rahab in heaven one day. I love her grit.

Rahab's people were on the brink of destruction. The city of Jericho was in the path of the Israelites, who had been taking the surrounding lands on their march to the promised land. The people of Jericho had heard whispers of divine intervention and impossible deeds performed by an unseen God. I imagine swirling discontentment and curiosity stirring within her: *Is there more to life than what I know?*

Scripture states that no one can come to God unless He first draws them (John 6:44). I have to believe that God was wooing her, stirring her, daring her to trust Him. How else can you explain her willingness to risk her life to hide the Jewish spies who came to her home in order to scope out the land? Why would she possess such courage, discernment, and boldness to side with the "enemies" who were about to destroy her city? Let's look at their exchange:

> Before the spies went to sleep that night, Rahab went up on the roof to talk with them. "I know the Lord has given you this land," she told them. "We are all afraid of you. Everyone in the land is living in terror. For we have heard how the Lord made a dry path for you through the Red Sea when you left Egypt. And we know what you did to Sihon and Og, the two Amorite kings east of the Jordan River, whose people you completely destroyed. No wonder our hearts have melted in fear! No one has the courage to fight after hearing such things. For the Lord your God is the supreme God of the heavens above and the earth below." (Joshua 2:8–11)

Rahab confirmed the prophetic promise of God to God's people. She said, "I know the Lord *has given you this land*." God awakened Rahab's heart of faith so that the stories of the Israelites' exploits meant something to her. Most others in that town simply cowered in fear. She rose up in faith, put feet to her faith, and took risks because of her faith!

From the risks she took for the spies, from the way she already knew of God's actions in the land, it's clear that Rahab (like my friend Ashley) had grown weary of her old life. She was ready for a change and desired a new life, one that required faith to embrace. In return for her help, the spies promised she would be spared from the destruction of the city (Joshua 2:14).

After forty years of wandering in the wilderness, a new generation of God's people was finally prepared to enter the promised land, and they had to go through Rahab's city to get there. Rahab would journey with them, rescued from destruction to walk into a new, redeemed life. A Gentile prostitute was woven into the fabric of God's story. Her descendant Boaz (a righteous, upstanding man of God) married Ruth (another outsider, a Moabite, regarded as an enemy of the Jewish people). Ruth and Boaz had a son named Obed, which means worshiper or servant of God. Because of God's indiscriminatory, rescuing love and Rahab's precious faith, we find righteous fruit in the family tree. And best of all, we find Rahab grafted into the lineage of Christ. This is an absolute miracle.

My friend Sheila Walsh writes, "God's love story is all about rescue. It doesn't happen on our schedule or the way we would have written it, but we can trust who He is. If there ever was a moment when we needed to grasp hold of that truth, surely it is now."[3]

Though we don't always understand God's ways or His timing, we can trust His heart. We *must* trust His heart. He is always and only good. Our God is amazing. He's continually on a wild rescue mission, seeking those whose hearts are turned toward Him. He didn't keep His distance from Ashley when she was on a self-destructive path, nor was He far from Rahab when she sold herself for a living. He was right there, ready to respond to their faith when they were ready to trust Him.

It's the same with you. And your loved ones who are far from God or on a path that's not His best for them. He's not far away. He's right here with you and right there with them. God is passionate and purposeful when it comes to rescue and redemption. It's what He does best.

Do you need rescuing? Long to see redemption in your story? He's right here! Call on His name! Ask Him to do for you what you cannot do for yourself.

God didn't save you to enslave you. He rescued you because He delights in you. He empowers you because He's redeeming you and reaching the world through you. You're a vessel of honor, set apart for a divine purpose. God desires for you to live a life entirely disproportionate to who you are. The only way that's possible is through God's intervention. He's ready and waiting for every heart that's prepared for Him.

> Though we don't always understand God's ways or His timing, we can trust His heart.

I love to say out loud for my own ears to hear: "The One who parted the Red Sea is alive in me!" Never forget that you serve a miracle-working, rescuing God. His miracles are not out of style or out of power. His promises are as potent as they've ever been. He's simply looking for those who dare to trust Him and take Him at His word.

Whatever you've experienced of God up to this point, whatever rescue stories you've watched unfold thus far, know this: There's more. So much more than you can imagine! May God so align you with His best purposes for you that you never run out of redemption stories. May He give you a front-row seat to watch as millions come to faith in Jesus and live wholeheartedly for Him. A great harvest awaits us.

PRAYER

Lord God Almighty,

Holy is Your name! Your kingdom come! Your will be done, in my life as it is in heaven.

I confess that I sometimes turn to quick fixes to numb my pain. I forget that You are the Redeemer of my story. I turn to You, look to You, and invite You afresh today to be Lord of my life.

Show me how to live worthy of Your name. Reveal the places in me that have settled for far less than Your best will for me. Take me higher, take me deeper, and awaken fresh wonder and faith in me.

In Jesus's name I pray, amen.

MOMENTS OF REFLECTION

1. Read Joshua 2:1–21 and reflect on Rahab's courage. It's often desperate situations that reveal what's inside us. What are your current circumstances showing you about yourself?

2. When Rahab decided to protect the spies (and side with the enemy), she did so because she believed God was the one true God. At that point, she had no idea how beautifully God would redeem her story. And neither do you or I. Spend a moment thanking God, by faith, for all He has planned for you.

3. Pray for the people in your life who still need to be rescued.

Chapter Six

GOD STRENGTHENS ME AND MOVES MY MOUNTAINS

When we hit our knees, we pick a fight with the enemy. We are immediately transported to the front lines of the kingdom, where we wage war with principalities and powers. That is where the battle is won or lost—on our knees! And when we hit our knees, God fights our battles for us.

MARK BATTERSON,
DRAW THE CIRCLE

"This is my command—be strong and courageous! Do not be afraid or discouraged. For the LORD your God is with you wherever you go."

JOSHUA 1:9

Have you ever faced an impossible situation and not known what to do? I remember when it felt like there was a wall of Jericho in my life that was so impenetrable, so impossibly immovable, that I had lost all hope. But our hearts can't survive without hope. I knew I needed to wrestle for and find a fresh faith perspective.

I cried out to God for answers, and He provided a strategy. He made no promises about the timing of my breakthrough. Still, He reminded me that His promises never fail and that my posture and perspective *will* affect even the most impossible situations. Also, if I choose fierce prayer and a faith perspective, it will not only *weaken* my Jericho wall but also deeply fortify and *strengthen* me.

Here's what He spoke to me. Perhaps it'll help you.

> *Susie, from now on, speak about this situation only in a redemptive way. Don't look back. Don't rehearse. Don't rehash. When you feel tempted to express hopeless thoughts from a despairing heart, hold your tongue. You'll find that unrestrained venting only weakens you.*
>
> *Allowing your mouth to run wild with angry or anxious thoughts throws your whole body out of whack. Instead, abide in Me. Draw your life strength from Me. I've got it to give. Look up and forward with faith and hope. Speak only from a place of faith, hope, and love. Life and death are in the power of the tongue (Proverbs 18:21). Use your words to bring life to this situation! Speak to your wall, speak to your mountain, and speak to your heart! I've entrusted and empowered you with Spirit-filled, life-giving words. Use them!*

Also, do not try to figure this out from your limited perspective. You'll get lost in the weeds. It's not going to make sense because it doesn't make sense. That's because there's something much deeper going on beneath the surface. I know what's on the other side of this wall. I see it all. You don't. Look above it. Keep entrusting this to Me. Keep looking to Me. You can trust Me. I don't miss a thing.

And finally, hold fast to your identity during this trial. You are highly favored and honored in the kingdom. This situation has no power to diminish who you are to Me. You are loved, called, equipped, and chosen. Walk forward with humble, bold confidence. I've got you. I'm with you. And I'll keep counseling you with My eye on you.

Let me tell you, friend, after years of contending, years of crying to God, my roots run deeper, and I am stronger. I know a few things about my flesh's tendency to self-protect, the Enemy's plan to discourage and derail, and God's intent to bless and strengthen His children.

Our battles must never be wasted on us. If God is not giving you what you want at the moment, it's because there's something you *need* in your current circumstance. In Psalm 32:8, the Lord promises this: "I will guide you along the best pathway for your life. I will advise you and watch over you." Look for the treasures. Look for the opportunities to trust God. Notice how often you're presented with a choice to choose love or fear, faith or despair. And choose wisely. When you choose faith, hope, and love, you're strengthened, and the Enemy's resolve is weakened.

JEN'S JERICHO WALL

Jen was raised in the church but strayed from God in her young adulthood. She met Brian at a bar, and they fell in love. A few months later,

Jen discovered she was pregnant. She married Brian, which led them into a cycle of toxic conflict. He liked control, and she had a short fuse, resulting in frequent fights. Jen threatened to leave numerous times but never followed through.

After about eleven years, Jen's love tank felt drained. One night, she went out with her girlfriends and complained about her husband; something shifted within her. The following day, she woke up and told him she was leaving the marriage. She was done.

Brian was devastated, but there was no changing her mind. They divorced. Over the next couple of years, they'd see each other at their kids' events. Brian often suggested they try to make it work for the kids, but neither walked with God, and Jen wasn't interested.

Three years after her divorce, God's voice thundered in Jen's heart while she was in the shower: *Go back before it's too late.* Feeling the presence of the Lord, Jen slid to the floor in a heap and began to weep. All the years of pain and heartache, poor choices, and missed opportunities bubbled up without condemnation. She sobbed as she turned toward the Lord, sensing His profound love and compassion, washing her clean and giving her new hope. Two hours passed with no words, only tears, yet in that moment on the bathroom floor, she remembered God and felt so grateful to trust Him again.

Suddenly, her spiritual root system activated, and she began to pursue God, read His Word, and listen for His voice. God provided her with specific guidance on pursuing Brian, including what to say, what not to say, and how best to serve. But this time, Brian was *not* interested. He was dating a woman he really liked and had moved on from his relationship with Jen. They'd been divorced for three years, after all.

But Jen persisted without being overbearing. She relied deeply on God for His protection and direction. He continually provided her with specific instructions, and when she doubted or felt heartsick from Brian's cold response, she heard the Lord whisper, *Just keep doing what I tell you to do.*

The more Jen obeyed, the stronger her faith grew. She continued to tell the Lord, "Whatever You tell me to do, I'll do it. Just don't let me make a mistake." Jen's mom faithfully interceded as well. One day, she shared this verse that offered Jen a new and fresh prayer strategy: "Jesus replied, 'Every plant not planted by my heavenly Father will be uprooted'" (Matthew 15:13).

Jen recognized that some individuals in Brian's life had poisoned his outlook and hardened his heart. Therefore, Jen knelt and prayed, "Father, I thank You for Your faithfulness to Your Word. Whatever You have not planted in Brian's life, You will uproot. I trust You."

She sent Brian texts letting him know she was praying for him. One day, she made him a meal and handed it to him when they exchanged their kids. She even asked if she could clean his house. Additionally, she filled his fridge with groceries. Every one of her efforts was met with a brick wall. Brian was like the walls of Jericho—unyielding, uninterested, and seemingly unresponsive to her gestures. But deep inside, and unknown to Jen, his resolve was crumbling.

Even more interesting was how God plucked people out of Brian's life when the time was right.

Jen asked Brian if they could meet with their counselor together. Up to this point, she'd been going alone. He said yes. But an hour before their appointment, he changed his plans and said he wasn't coming. Jen said, "If you don't come to this appointment, I'm done. I've done what God asked me to do. This counselor hears and listens to the Holy Spirit. I listen to the Holy Spirit. If the counselor says it's time to be done, I'll be done." Brian decided to keep the appointment.

Jen and Brian sat down with the counselor. He looked at Jen (not knowing what she had just said to Brian on the phone), paused, and then said, "Jen, be done. No more texting. No more emails. Do not ask him for anything anymore." Then he turned to Brian and said, "Brian, this is a woman of God. God has transformed her life. He has a good man for her. I'm not sure what you'll do, but she's a good one."

Jen got in her car, drove away, and wept endless tears. She told the Lord, "Lord, I did what You told me to do. I did what You asked, and it didn't turn out the way I thought it would. No matter what, though, it's me and You. I know I have You." Jen knew that God was her best friend, and He would never forsake her, and she was going to be okay.

Fifteen minutes later, Brian called Jen, asking if they could gather as a family that weekend. They started dating and kept themselves pure, as if dating for the first time. They followed God's lead this time and remarried within two months. That was eleven years ago. They are both passionate about God, and their family has been restored.

Jen said, "Whatever I was willing to hand over to God determined how big and fast He could work. The more I surrendered, the more access He had to my story. He's not looking for perfect. He's looking for willing. He's looking for our *yes*."

An added blessing to this miracle is how God protected and restored their children. They all can look back to those few years of the divorce and say, "It's as if it never happened."

God can do that, you know. Embrace the possibility that God will not only bring down your Jericho wall, but He'll restore your situation so completely that it feels as if the struggle never happened. Anything is possible.

Author and pastor Tim Timberlake writes:

> If you're feeling overwhelmed right now, give this a try. Focus on

God's love for you for a couple of minutes, allowing his acceptance and approval to give you peace. Remind yourself that even if all else fails, you still have God. You still have heaven. You still have his love. Then begin to think of people close to you. Set aside your own hurt (not permanently, but just for a moment) and ask yourself what it would look like to love those people more today. Can you help them? Can you serve them? Can you encourage them? Let your perspective shift and your posture relax. If you can love, you'll be okay.[1]

> Embrace the possibility that God will not only bring down your Jericho wall, but He'll restore your situation so completely that it feels as if the struggle never happened.

JOSHUA'S HEART PREPARED FOR BATTLE

At the beginning of the book of Joshua, God tasked Joshua with finally leading the Israelites into the promised land, after all their years of wandering. God told Joshua to be strong and courageous, not to fear or fret. Why? Because the Lord was on Joshua's side! If God is for you, who can stand against you? But then, in chapter five we read this exchange:

> When Joshua was near the town of Jericho, he looked up and saw a man standing in front of him with sword in hand. Joshua went up to him and demanded, "Are you friend or foe?"
>
> "Neither one," he replied. "I am the commander of the Lord's army."

PAUSE.

BREATHE.

PONDER.

How has your current battle
strengthened you?

Is what you're doing working?
Is it time for a new strategy?

Listen for God's voice; do what He says.

God will do what He does best.

He will come through for you.

> At this, Joshua fell with his face to the ground in reverence. "I am at your command," Joshua said. "What do you want your servant to do?"
>
> The commander of the LORD's army replied, "Take off your sandals, for the place where you are standing is holy." And Joshua did as he was told. (vv. 13–15)

If God told Joshua that He was on Joshua's side, why didn't this commander also tell Joshua, "I'm a friend. I'm on your side"? It's one thing to put your unwavering trust in the Lord; it's another to presume upon God. Though Joshua's heart was all in, the Israelites still had wandering hearts. After all God had done for them, some still had idols in their tents!

The angel reminded Joshua that though God is with us, *we're the ones on the Lord's side*; not the other way around. He sets the terms, He guides our way, and He gets the say. When we fail, He loves us still. When we're unfaithful, He remains faithful. But sometimes we need a spiritual reset—a reminder of just who it is that we serve. He is the God of Angel Armies, and we should take Him seriously.[2]

Humility and holiness precede victory, while pride and irreverence precede a fall. Before Joshua marched into battle, God had him take off his shoes. Often, before the Lord brings a breakthrough in our circumstances—before He tears down the wall or moves the mountain—He first dismantles our pride, ego, and self-justifying, self-protective ways. He tenderizes our hearts so we're more apt to listen and obey, which is critical in battle if we hope to win against the Enemy of our souls. If the Enemy can find an unattended gate into our souls, he'll take it, and a kingdom divided cannot stand.

It's interesting how our battles, if we allow them, strengthen and tenderize us. On one hand, we develop resilience and endurance, which are essential for our spiritual growth. On the other hand, we're humbled, reminded that we cannot take a step or a breath without almighty God breathing His life in and through us.

JERICHO'S WALLS

What does it look like for God to fight our battles for us? We get a glimpse in the battle of Jericho.

The people of Jericho heard about the power and influence of almighty God. Though Jericho was shut tight behind fortified walls, God told the Israelites to march around the city walls *in silence*, once a day for six days. Then, on the seventh day, they were to march around the city seven times, blow the ram's horn, let out a mighty shout, and watch the walls come tumbling down.

Jericho was a fortified city with towering walls, its gates tightly closed out of *fear.* I highlight this point to suggest that someone may be grappling with their own fears on the other side of your Jericho wall. Understanding this may help you to know how to pray for them.

Read the story in Joshua 6, and you may scratch your head and wonder: *Why those specific instructions? March around the city of Jericho once a day for six days? What?* Imagine the people inside the city. In fear, they ducked behind the wall when they heard the warriors' footsteps. But nothing happened. No voices, no battle cries. They just marched around the city. Then they left. Did they lose heart? Go home? Change their minds? And why did Joshua insist that they remain silent as they marched (6:10)?

I'm no scholar, but my guess is that because their ancestors were known grumblers and complainers, Joshua wanted a sanctified victory.

He didn't want them to utter a word, especially whining words of complaint, the same way God didn't want me to indulge in venting and complaining when I was facing my Jericho wall. They were on a mission and taking their orders from God alone. The only sound they heard was the blast of the ram's horn as the priests blew with all their might.

Again, picture the people inside the city. Every day, for six days, they wake up and wonder what will happen, only to find the silent army marching around their city. Why weren't they making a move? And what's with the ram's horns?

Did people inside the walls of Jericho mock them? Throw stones at them? Or were they cowering in fear? Imagine the restraint of the Israelites, sticking with the plan and following their orders. Did their silent resolve weaken their enemy and strengthen them? I think so.

Finally, on the seventh day, the orders changed. God's people were to march around the city seven times in one day, and the priests were to blow their horns with all their might. When the priests gave one long blast on the ram's horn, all the people were to shout at the top of their lungs. Imagine the horns blasting, the people shouting, and suddenly, the walls crumbling down. This happened!

They didn't fire a weapon. They didn't pummel the walls with shovels. They didn't lob cannonballs over the wall. They marched around the wall and let God do the rest.

Some say that the walls of Jericho fell outward, creating ramps that led into the city.[3]

Your resolve and willingness to take your marching orders from God alone could, right now, be *strengthening you and weakening your Jericho wall*. What if the very thing that stands in your way becomes the ramp to your breakthrough?

My friend Mark Batterson writes:

> What if the very thing that stands in your way becomes the ramp to your breakthrough?

> If you are on God's side, then God is on your side. God will fight for you as you fight for Him. And you can live with holy confidence, knowing that when God is contending for your cause, your cause is destined to succeed. This doesn't mean there won't be setbacks and sacrifices along the way; it just means the war has already been won. Prayer is the difference between you fighting for God and God fighting for you.[4]

Your job is to keep your heart in obedience and stay humble, teachable, and reverent before God. His is to strengthen and encourage you, to give you strategy, direction, and protection. He knows where you're weak and where you're strong. When you know deep in your bones that you need Him every hour, and you keep responding to His transformative work within you, and then you pray and believe from *that place*, that's when you'll see mountains move, walls crumble, and hearts restored.

Remember my friend Jen, whose impossible Jericho wall came tumbling down? She stopped by my house the other day. She and her husband and kids are enjoying their lives together, trusting God together, and becoming the best versions of themselves together. I can't tell you what it does for my heart to see her living in her healed and redeemed story.

I'm still waiting for my Jericho wall to come down. And she knows it. She put her hands on my shoulders, looked me in the eyes, and reminded me to keep hope alive, to keep praying persistently, and to keep doing whatever God asks me to do. He'll do the rest.

Then she added, "I see you getting stronger in the process." And it's true. I am.

How about you? Is your wall shaking yet? Even if it doesn't seem to be budging, can you see that God is transforming you as you continue to trust Him with your impossible situation? He strengthens you as you trust Him. And He's the One—when the time is right—who can change your story in a moment.

> "If you remain in me and my words remain in you, you may ask for anything you want, and it will be granted!" (John 15:7)

He can make a way where there is no way. He can make up for lost time and restore what the Enemy has stolen. He's a miracle-working God and He's working a miracle in you while you wait.

PRAYER

Lord God Almighty,

I want to live such a sanctified, redeemed, all-in life where I see miracles all around me. Fill me afresh with Your Spirit! Show me what You want from me.

I know that the more I surrender to You, the more I'll see You work in my life. I can trust You! You know what's on the other side of my Jericho wall. You are a miracle-working God.

Change me, Lord. Strengthen me. Give me divine strategy to know how to take my stand and watch You work. And, when the time is right, move my mountains, tear down the walls, and bring the breakthrough!

In Jesus's name I pray, amen.

MOMENTS OF REFLECTION

1. Read Joshua 1:1–9 and ask God to personalize it for you. What is He saying to you right now, in your current circumstances?

2. What might strength and courage look like in your situation?

3. Are you holding fast to your identity while you wait for your breakthrough?

Chapter Seven

GOD OWES ME NOTHING BUT GIVES ME EVERYTHING

The holiness of God, divinity uncloaked, is too much for us. It would be like staring at the sun. Times ten thousand. Throughout Scripture, people who have encountered Jesus share a common reaction. A common posture. They are undone. They repent. They fall on their face because they know, maybe for the very first time, their own unworthiness in the sight of such perfect holiness.

CHARLES MARTIN,
IT IS FINISHED

> "I had only heard about you before,
> but now I have seen you with my own eyes.
> I take back everything I said,
> and I sit in dust and ashes to show my repentance."
>
> JOB 42:5–6

Do you remember where you were when you first realized—deep down in your bones—that God is God, and you are not? When you understood that God is so much bigger, His love so much deeper, and His power so much greater than your limited mind can grasp, and your knees buckled? Do you recall how small you felt, yet how loved you knew you were? Oh, to have more encounters like that! If you've never had such an experience, I pray you will. Soon!

In my book *Closer Than Your Next Breath*, I tell the following story:

> One day, while crammed in a van with a bunch of other college students on our way home for the weekend, I curled up with a book by Watchman Nee. I don't recall the title, but I do remember what happened. I went from being half involved with the surrounding conversations and partially attuned to what I was reading to suddenly focusing on the words on the page.
>
> At that moment, I had an encounter with God unlike anything I had ever experienced up to that point. His Spirit drew near, and I could not hide from Him. Like a movie reel,

God is so much bigger, His love so much deeper, and His power so much greater than your limited mind can grasp.

I saw my life's story unfold. I saw my life in fast motion, one deed after another, and the motivations that fueled my actions. A consistent theme ran throughout my life. Everything I'd done—good, bad, and otherwise—was to rescue my sense of self-worth. Most of my good deeds were to prove myself. Most sinful indulgences were to escape from myself. *I didn't know who I was, so I wasted precious time, treasure, and talents.*

Though God can and did redeem every aspect of my story, all my strivings were wasted efforts. I'd misused my time, treasure, and talents to prove something that Jesus had already done, had already won. I didn't know any better then. But I did now. In that van I came face-to-face with the truth about my depravity and the power of God's holy standard for me.

There would be no dabbling in this walk of faith. God was not one to be trifled with. He wasn't messing around. I couldn't escape Him. I gasped. I trembled. I covered my mouth with my hands and tears escaped my eyes. Friends asked if I was okay, and I could only shake my head. I couldn't speak. I dared not justify my ways. I was guilty of selfish, self-preserving efforts. Though I had reason to be painfully insecure, I learned that security is just another form of selfishness. Self-preservation and kingdom life are entirely incompatible.[1]

Often, we experience these divine moments when we need an upgrade on our identity, a reset on our purpose, and, most importantly, a fresh revelation of who God is. He intends for us to progress from strength to strength, glory to glory, shining ever brighter until the full light of day (Proverbs 4:18). And almost always, in these moments, God invites us to a new level of surrender, humility, and trust. *There's always so much more of God to experience.*

> God invites us to a new level of surrender, humility, and trust. *There's always so much more of God to experience.*

Though facing your humanity is sobering and humbling, it's also sacred and beautiful. You suddenly realize how small you are and how great God is. You're in His tender care, on His mind, and in His heart. You are one of God's best ideas, and He is deeply committed to your life story. Anything you're white-knuckling right now is best left in His hands. Any striving, proving, or fighting for your rights will leave you overwhelmed and under-joyed. What if you opened your hands right now and trusted Him with the hardest parts of your story? Sometimes, complete surrender and heartfelt worship are the best forms of spiritual warfare.

GOD OWNS EVERYTHING

In the early 1960s, Otto Koning served as a missionary in New Guinea. He had a garden there where nothing survived. His land and the hearts of the people both seemed like barren, hardened soil. To make matters worse, the natives were chronic thieves. They stole *everything*.

One day, Otto noticed that his can opener had gone missing. Otto and his wife used a machete to open their canned goods. Then, another day, Otto spotted a woman in the village wearing his can opener around her neck as a necklace. A similar thing happened with their diaper pins, which the village women used as earrings.

This scenario occurred repeatedly: A few of the locals knocked on Otto's front door to start a conversation (to distract him), while others snuck into the backyard to steal his clothes from the clothesline. Otto went from despair to anger. He tried to preach the gospel, but his words fell flat because he was always so angry. The locals called him "the angry white man." When he preached the gospel and talked about being a Christian, they said they'd like to meet one sometime. This poked Otto's conscience, but he felt stuck in an impossible situation.

After many tries, Otto finally found something he could grow in his garden: pineapples. They thrived in that soil! But as soon as a fresh crop of pineapples appeared, the locals stole them, leaving his garden desolate. No matter what Otto said or did, he couldn't stop the thieves or get any traction in his missionary work.

One day Otto traveled back to the States to attend a conference. The speaker said something like, "Give your possessions to God. He takes good care of His property. Whatever gift you give to God with the right motives, you will never lack in that area. Whatever aspect of your life you give to God, He will do a better job with it than you can. The people you argue with, you will never win for Christ. If you keep fighting for your rights, you will destroy your health."

Otto was deeply affected. He began to weep and confessed, *God, that's exactly what I've done.* The speaker then asked, "How many of you need to give something to God tonight? To surrender control?" Otto raised his hand and said, "God, it's Your pineapple garden now. Do whatever You want with it." Suddenly, God's peace enveloped Otto's entire being. The burden lifted from his shoulders. He felt as if he was born again, all over again.

Otto returned to the jungle and declared the pineapple garden belonged to God. Soon, the pineapples grew more robust than ever before. And still, the locals stole them without considering Otto's feelings. He'd look out his window and wave to the locals as they stole from him. His joy returned. He trusted God for what he needed. Some men asked him one day if he'd become a Christian. "Why do you ask?" Otto inquired.

They replied, "Because you're not angry anymore." Again, Otto felt deeply convicted that his anger had so diminished his witness.

Meanwhile, something supernatural was happening in the local village. And not in a good way. Months had passed since Otto gave up his right to his garden. When the locals learned that Otto no longer owned the garden, they panicked. "Who owns the garden now? Who are we stealing from now?" They hoped it wasn't their local witch doctor. They knocked on Otto's door and demanded to know who owned the garden.

Otto shared that he had turned over his garden to God. They cried out, "Tell Him you want it back! Take the garden back! We don't want to steal from your God!"

Otto replied, "I'm so happy *not* to own that garden anymore. I finally feel better, and I have joy."

Unfortunately, the villagers were experiencing something entirely different. Since they began stealing from God, nothing had gone well in the village. The rain wouldn't fall, their gardens wouldn't grow, they couldn't catch fish, and their women weren't becoming pregnant. They feared that their enemies would soon outnumber them.

They audaciously told Otto, "We never permitted you to give your garden to your God. Take it back!" They pulled out their spears and pointed them at Otto.

He asked the people, "Why don't you just stop stealing from God?" Otto shared that these people had never faced a temptation and not yielded. Satan controlled them completely.

Then things took a sudden turn.

One of the villagers stepped forward and shared his perspective with his people. "It seems you can't be a Christian and own a garden at the same time. If you can't leave his pineapples alone, go the other way. Let his God own them. Then he can be a Christian. Let's allow him to be a Christian."

The villagers looked at Otto and asked, "Does your God see in the dark?" Otto nodded yes. They realized that God doesn't miss a thing. They said, "Your God is big, isn't He?"

Otto again agreed and continued, "He controls whether your wife gets pregnant or if you catch fish. You can't breathe without God's help."

Half the villagers decided to stop stealing pineapples that day, while the other half continued their thievery. Then, something strange occurred. Those who no longer stole from Otto came to Christ. They took Otto's pineapples, presented them to him, and said, "Please take these into your house. We can't bear to see our people stealing your pineapples." They even stood guard around his garden.[2]

> "The thief approaches *with malicious intent*, looking to steal, slaughter, and destroy; I came to give life with joy and abundance."
> (John 10:10 The Voice)

Wherever you are contending, whatever is causing you angst, surrender it all to the Lord. It's His burden, His battle. God owes us nothing, but when we surrender our all to Him, He gives us everything.

Only the false identity grabs for itself. Our truest identity—our God-given, Spirit-filled identity—trusts and knows that God owns it all and takes good care of His children. "His righteousness will be like a garden in early spring, with plants springing up everywhere" (Isaiah 61:11). Want to see life spring up all around you? Give God your garden. Give Him the hurts others have inflicted upon you. Give Him the debt they owe you. Trust Him to make it right, to take care of your precious heart, and to bring justice and vindication when the time is right.

PAUSE.

BREATHE.

PONDER.

Do you long for a fresh encounter with God?

Open your hands and surrender that thing you're holding on to.

The people who've hurt you?

Entrust them to the One who judges correctly (1 Peter 2:23).

Trust Him. Receive His peace.

Rest in His care.

JOB'S SURRENDER

Often when you hear stories of people who've walked through prolonged, unrelenting trials and surrendered them to God, you'll hear someone reference the trials of Job. It's hard to understand why God allowed Satan to inflict such pain and loss on Job, and hard to fathom how Job kept handing everything over to God, but we're still talking about this story today, and there's much we can learn from it.

Job was a righteous, God-fearing man. His devotion ran deep. How do we know? When Job endured his first unimaginable series of crises (the loss of his children, farmhands, and animals), Job's instinctive response was to fall to the ground to worship: "I came naked from my mother's womb, and I will be naked when I leave. The Lord gave me what I had, and the Lord has taken it away. Praise the name of the Lord!" (Job 1:21). Scripture says, "In all of this, Job did not sin by blaming God" (v. 22).

Wow. What? How is it that a man's response to such unfathomable loss is to bow in worship and offer God open-handed surrender? You know, Job didn't arrive there overnight. He lived his blessed, beautiful life in complete surrender to God. Yes, he enjoyed health and wealth, but he didn't hoard it. He shared his blessings with the lost, the lowly, and the overlooked. He helped widows and orphans and stood up for the voiceless (29:12–16; 31:16–18). He didn't remain silent in the face of injustice, because he feared and honored God (31:34). Job was a truly righteous man. Even God said so. Here's what the Lord said about him:

> "Have you noticed my servant Job? He is the finest man in all the earth. He is blameless—a man of complete integrity. He fears God and stays away from evil." (1:8)

Some people are all show and no "go." Their facade makes them appear more righteous than they truly are. Even their good deeds are transactional. Not Job. God sees and knows all hearts, and He declared Job to be the earth's finest.

Then Job's story spiraled into the deepest levels of pain and loss. While his friends initially appeared wonderful by coming to see him and remaining silent, they couldn't help themselves after a while.

We all reveal what we're made of over time when pushed far enough. Job's friends cherished their formulas and took pride in their ability to assess and diagnose pain and suffering (Job 4–23). Jesus, on the other hand, was always moved with compassion when He saw the suffering crowds (whether the suffering was their fault or not). Jesus led with compassion, not explanations.

When you encounter a suffering person and instinctively attempt to diagnose why this happened to them, you're dealing in formulas, not in faith. This is the opposite of surrender. Yes, some people suffer because they've made poor choices. But God's grace is endless, and He'll leave the ninety-nine to rescue the one who has wandered into the ditch, even if they dragged themselves there (Matthew 18:12). That's how Jesus is. That's who Jesus is.

Jesus led with compassion, not explanations.

Job's problems were not Job's fault. Job's "friends" were mistaken in their assessments (and a little later in the story, you'll find that God was not happy with them). If you zoom out, you'll notice that Job's friends had some wise things to say, but they spoke out of context and without love. They puffed up their chests, accused Job of sin, and presumed to speak for God. To declare truth with pride (and without love) is to cut another person deeply.

Yet God allowed this injustice for a season. Why? I mentioned this earlier, but I'll repeat it here: *We all reveal what we're made of over time when pushed far enough*. What's in us spills out when the pressure is on. If you jump ahead in the book of Job to chapters 27 through 31, you see Job defending his own honor and righteousness. Anyone in Job's position would do so, right? I'd think so!

But here's where we go astray. When our righteous acts become defining acts for us—gestures that not only prove our worth but prove that God owes us something—we're standing on shaky ground. Yes, God is taken with our obedience; He records our actions for a future reward. Our righteous deeds are a holy offering to a righteous and holy God. They're not insurance or a quid pro quo agreement that guarantees we won't suffer.

If or when we pull out our self-righteous ID card that lists all the good things we've done, and we hold it up to God as our defense, we're out of line, and God must confront us. And confront Job, God did.

Jump ahead to chapters 38 through 41 and hear the thundering voice of the Almighty ask Job where he was when God formed the earth, told the water where to stop and the land to begin. Or if he had any idea where a horse gets its strength or an ostrich its wingspan. Could Job command an eagle to spread its wings and soar through the skies? Can any of us command creation to obey or arrange the stars in the sky? Or make the sun stand still in the sky? Only God!

Job responded to God as you imagine he would.

> "You asked, 'Who is this that questions my wisdom with
> such ignorance?'
> It is I—and I was talking about things I knew
> nothing about,
> things far too wonderful for me.
> You said, 'Listen and I will speak!

> I have some questions for you,
> and you must answer them.'
> I had only heard about you before,
> but now I have seen you with my own eyes.
> I take back everything I said,
> and I sit in dust and ashes to show my repentance."
> (42:3–6)

God was angry at Job's friends because they spoke incorrectly about Him—unlike Job, God's precious, suffering servant who regained a proper view of God amid his profound time of testing. While Job was still in physical agony, God asked him to pray for those who had only added to his pain (42:8–9). Imagine how that would feel. But Job had just encountered God and did not hesitate to obey Him, unaware of how his story would unfold. In his sick body, Job prayed for his healthy, self-righteous friends.

God restored Job to even greater glory than before (v. 10). He doubled Job's portion, and Job's later years were far more blessed than his former years. Imagine how Job must have stewarded his later years, so blessed, at rest, and fully aware that God owed him nothing but gave him everything.

THE WORSHIP GOD DESERVES

God is magnificent, miraculous, and meticulous. He's attentive to the finest details and sovereign over all creation. He gives man his free will. He's only a prayer away and wants to redeem every part of our story.

God gave us everything when He gave us His Son to die in our place. Jesus gave us everything when He defeated sin, sickness, and death on the cross *for us*. He gave us His precious, powerful Holy Spirit to infuse our lives with power, conviction, and authority. God provides His defense against our Enemy. The Father, Son, and Holy Spirit have secured our eternity, and nothing and no one can snatch us out of His hand or separate us from His love. God gives and continues to give.

Even when the storms of life feel like they'll overtake us, God is for us. Even when people proudly misdiagnose our pain or wrongly assess our hardship, God is for us. Even when we stumble into the ditch by our own doing, God is with us, for us, and leading us back to our path of redemption. Because God is for us and Jesus is alive in us, we are more secure than our hearts can fathom.

God gives and continues to give.

Suffering doesn't weaken our worth, and our messy responses to the hardships of life don't diminish His love. Life on earth is hard. But God is so very good, patient, kind, and faithful. He's working everything out for your good and for His glory. Stay humble. Stay teachable. Develop a lifestyle of holy surrender. Trust God with every aspect of your life—especially the parts you're trying hardest to control. You're going to be okay. You can trust Him because of these encouraging words:

> What then shall we say to all these things? If God is for us, who can be [successful] against us? He who did not spare [even] His own Son, but gave Him up for us all, how will He not also, along with Him, graciously give us all things? Who will bring any charge against God's elect (His chosen ones)? It is God who justifies us [declaring us blameless and putting us in a right relationship with Himself]. Who is the one who condemns us? Christ Jesus is the One who died [to pay our penalty], and more than that, who was

> raised [from the dead], and who is at the right hand of God interceding [with the Father] for us. (Romans 8:31–34 AMP)

We can't breathe without God. Every day, He lavishes His love on us in a thousand different ways. Most of which go unnoticed or unacknowledged by us. Yet it's in our worship, with grateful hearts, that we see God most clearly. When we stretch out our hands in praise because there is no one like Him, we find our home in Him and our hearts rest in Him. Our vision clears, and we live as the redeemed saints we were always meant to be.

Pastor Samuel Rodriguez writes:

> You don't praise because of a feeling but because of a filling! When you are filled by the same Spirit who raised Jesus from the dead, you know that all things work together for your good according to God's all-knowing plans. When you are filled by the same Spirit who descended on believers in the Upper Room, you know that you have supernatural power to endure natural disaster, personal crisis, family turmoil, and devastating loss. Why? Because you choose to trust God even when you don't understand all that's going on around you. *Because you believe His promises will be fulfilled.* Because you know the same Spirit dwells in you.[3]

One of the signs we're maturing in our faith and deepening in our knowledge of God is when we spend so much time with God, getting to know His character, that the Enemy loses every time he tempts us to accuse God of something he himself is guilty of. Our safest, most beautiful place is in the heart of our Beloved—trusting His love, relying on His goodness, and counting on His promises. Hard seasons are only for a season. Every blessing and every battle is packed with eternal possibilities and the opportunity to trust the redeeming power of our intimate, kind, mighty, and all-powerful God.

If there's anything in you that wants to stand on your own efforts, righteousness, or service, I ask you to humbly bow, open your hands, and give God the glory He deserves. Ask Him for a fresh revelation of who He is. Like Job, ponder His handiwork in nature—in the butterfly, the eagle, and the lionfish. Stand in awe when the sun rises and sing a song of faithfulness when the sun sets at the end of the day.

There's only one God. You bear His image. But He alone is God. He owes us nothing but gives us everything—eternity, life with Him, tears wiped away, everlasting joy, and then some. We're truly the most blessed of all creation.

When you keep in the forefront of your mind that you are a child of God, when you remember the lengths to which He went to prove His love, to save your soul, and to establish your purpose, then you will become a worshiping, grateful saint. Remembering what God has done for you, pondering what He has planned for you, holding fast to what He has promised you, and *living from that reality* will help you become the image-bearer God always knew you would be.

PRAYER

God in heaven,

Holy is Your name! Your kingdom come, Your will be done in me, around me, and through me!

Forgive me for the countless subtle (and sometimes blatant) ways I shift my weight onto my works and expect You to do what I want You to do. You are God, and I am not! All of who I am is meant to be a holy offering to You. And so, I lift up my hands, and I sing a new song to You today.

Purify my heart. Strengthen my frame. Heal my soul. And make me whole. It's my greatest joy and honor to be Your child.

Thank You, Lord.

Amen.

MOMENTS OF REFLECTION

1. Job was being pressed on all sides. He was suffering, grieving, and dealing with his pompous, accusatory friends. He was trying to defend his honor against men who were wrongly accusing him. Read Job 19:25–27. How do you think he kept going?

2. How do you strengthen yourself in the Lord when you feel misunderstood by man?

3. What do you need to surrender to the Lord in this season of life?

Chapter Eight

GOD ALWAYS SPEAKS A BETTER WORD

You are a beloved family member of God, and because of that you are given a seat at the table with Almighty God.

LOUIE GIGLIO, *DON'T GIVE THE ENEMY A SEAT AT YOUR TABLE*

You have come to Mount Zion, to the city of the living God, to the heavenly Jerusalem, to heavenly messengers unnumbered, *to a joyful feast*, to the assembly of the firstborn registered as heaven's citizens, to God the righteous Judge of all, and to the spirits of all the righteous who have been perfected.

HEBREWS 12:22–23 THE VOICE

If I asked you to tell me some of the memorable things people have said to you over the years, how many were life-draining, hurtful, or even a little bit crazy? Why is it that the negative words imprint so deeply upon our hearts?

When I was in the throes of Lyme disease (before I knew it was Lyme), I had a friend who was tired of my trials. When the scary neurological symptoms first emerged, she put her hand on her hip, rolled her eyes, and said, "Now this? If it's not one thing with you, it's another. You know? I heard it's personalities like yours that most often get MS." My mouth dropped open, and I gulped down a gallon of fear. She turned and left, and I was alone with my terror. We both knew a woman from church whose body constantly tremored from multiple sclerosis. In her compassion fatigue, my friend hit me where it hurt.

Years later, when I was working in full-time ministry (writing and speaking), God opened the door for me to work in radio. I had served as a guest host before and loved it. I'm an introvert; I love books and one-on-one conversations. Radio suited me perfectly. Other authors and editors warned that I'd jeopardize my writing career by going behind the microphone because I would highlight everyone else's books and never have time to write my own. I considered their caution but felt so led by God that if He wanted me to lay my writing on the altar, I would. The peace of God was guiding me in this direction. If I was finished with writing books, I would trust God with that. But I wanted to make a wise decision. I was chatting to a friend about it while standing in the lobby at church when I noticed a woman listening in on what we were saying. She stepped into our conversation, put her hand on her hip, looked at me with total irritation, and said, "Radio? Why would *you* want to work in radio? You don't have a voice for it."

I suppose I could write several chapters on the careless words people have spoken to me that I've allowed to sink in. I'm sure you could as well. Most people who spew petty, controlling, or hurtful things are speaking from their own unresolved pain. An unhealed soul will always produce a skewed perspective. But if we allow someone's pain to diminish our purpose, we're in part responsible. We need to know what God says about us, what God has promised us, and how God's Word triumphs over man's puny perspective.

The problem isn't that people say things, because they will. The greater issue is that we allow these statements to linger unchallenged within our souls, and they keep lying to us. Without realizing it, we sometimes form narratives based on words spoken to us that are out of alignment with the better word that God speaks over us.

The more we advance in the kingdom, the more diligently we must guard (and sometimes challenge) our perspective. We must proactively decide which words can go in and which ones we must toss by the wayside.

An unhealed soul will always produce a skewed perspective.

GOD'S WORD MUST BE THE FINAL WORD

Many years ago, when my friend Melissa was first pregnant, she found a passage in Scripture that leaped off the page at her.

> "Bring all the tithes into the storehouse so there will be enough food

> in my Temple. If you do," says the LORD of Heaven's Armies, "I will open the windows of heaven for you. I will pour out a blessing so great you won't have enough room to take it in! Try it! Put me to the test! Your crops will be abundant, for I will guard them from insects and disease. Your grapes will not fall from the vine before they are ripe," says the LORD of Heaven's Armies. (Malachi 3:10–11)

Melissa and her husband were a young married couple starting a family. They felt called to tithe faithfully. When she read this passage from Malachi, one line especially reverberated through her soul: "Your grapes will not fall from the vine before they are ripe." Melissa placed her hand on her growing abdomen and thanked the Lord for keeping her baby in the womb until he was ready to be born.

One Sunday, a woman approached Melissa and forcefully said, "God told me something about your baby. God told me that your baby is coming six weeks early."

Melissa stepped back, placed a protective hand on her womb, and said, "What? Why would God say that? He's given me a promise. We're praying according to the promise." Even so, the woman's boldness unnerved Melissa. She walked away flustered and a little off-balance.

Every Sunday, that same woman beelined for Melissa to bring her this same word. And each week, Melissa's resolve weakened, and her fear increased.

About ten weeks before her due date, Melissa thought she was experiencing Braxton-Hicks contractions. They started slow but increased in intensity. It felt like her body was preparing for an early delivery. She went to the doctor, and sure enough, her cervix was thinning, and she was dilating. Feeling afraid and shaken, Melissa left her doctor's office, unsure what was happening or why.

A colleague and friend called Melissa and said, "You've been heavy on my heart. What's going on? How can I pray for you?" Melissa shared the promise God had given her, the words that had been spoken to her, and the fact that her body was preparing for an early delivery.

What Melissa's friend said next changed her prayer life. She said, "Melissa, that woman spoke a curse over you! And by not taking authority over it, your body is starting to align with it. Take authority over her words and apply God's promise to your life instead!"

Melissa shared with me, "I didn't know I had the right, let alone the responsibility, to take such a stand, but somehow, I knew my friend spoke truth. It felt consistent with my motherly instinct to protect my baby." So, together, they renounced that declaration and reclaimed the promise God had given them from the beginning.

The following Sunday, the woman marched up to Melissa, but before she could open her mouth, Melissa put up her hand like a stop sign and said, "Stop, and do not open your mouth. You will not speak to me about me or my baby. I don't want to hear a word." Then Melissa pointed across the room. "You see that man over there? He's my husband. If you think you have a word for me, go to him and he will decide. But as for me, I'm cutting you off. No more words to me about me or my baby."

Melissa felt something shift inside, and she knew she was standing on the truth. Over the next few days, all early signs of labor ceased. And when do you suppose Melissa gave birth to her firstborn son, Elisha? *Exactly on his due date.*

What's even more marvelous about her story is that Melissa got pregnant again, and her beautiful son Isaiah was born *on his due date.* In fact, *Melissa delivered all five of her children on their due dates.* Her doctor had never seen anything like it.

It's as if God wanted to make a statement: *I. Keep. My. Promises.*

Author and pastor Joby Martin writes:

What is the miracle you need? Name it. Write it out. Don't be afraid. *You have not because you ask not* (James 4:2). So, let's name the need and ask Him. This is not "name it and claim it." It's name it and lay it at the feet of Jesus and trust Him. Is it addiction? Cancer? Marriage? Prodigal? What? Maybe you think your problem is too big for Him? He defeated death, hell, and the grave. He can handle whatever you bring Him. So, let's bring the need and cry out for a miracle. *Let us come boldly before His throne of grace asking to receive mercy and grace to help us in our time of need* (Hebrews 4:16).[1]

All too often we settle for far less than God's best for us because someone spoke a word over our lives and we left it there unchallenged. Those negative, limiting beliefs seeped into our soil and we lost expectancy. But then one day God speaks to us through His Word, a sermon, a song, or a friend, and suddenly *life* quickens within us. We somehow *know* that we're made for *more*.

All too often we settle for far less than God's best for us because someone spoke a word over our lives and we left it there unchallenged.

Mind if I speak such a word over you today?

May the lies that still linger and the labels that still limit suddenly feel as untrue as they are. May you fling aside those spoken words and wholeheartedly receive the words that God speaks over you. You are His beloved, His child, His co-heir with Christ. You have all the resources of heaven on your side. You lack no good thing because you belong to Him. God wants to do a new thing in you!

EVERY PROMISE IS A PROPHECY

I was backstage with Anne Graham Lotz a few years ago because we were both guests on the *Life Today* show. After we taped our show segments, we recorded a few devotional thoughts for them to use for promotional purposes. I sat off to the side while they recorded Anne's segment. Anne is so dignified and grounded in God's Word. With her Bible in her lap, she looked into the camera and said, "Every promise is a prophecy." Her words quickened my heart.

Many have taken this idea way out of context and turned their walk with God into one transaction after another. But that's not what Anne was saying here. The Word of God is true. And it's living and breathing and powerful (Hebrews 4:12). God speaks through His Word.

If you're truly seeking God and deeply imprinting His Word on your heart, there will be times in His presence when He'll lift a word off the page, and you'll know it's for you. That's the living breath of God speaking to you! If He's made a promise, hold fast and strong to it. His promises are backed by the honor of His name (Psalm 138:2). He will likely fulfill His Word in a way that's different from what you expect, but trust Him. You will no doubt face the Enemy and lots of opposition, but trust in God. You may encounter jealous people who are threatened by your fierce faith and purposeful focus, but set your face like flint and hold on to God's Word.

We get into trouble when we close our eyes, swipe through our pages, and pick a promise. Or, before ever hearing from God, we decide what God will or will not do for us. We don't dictate to God; He dictates to us. But He's good to us. He speaks to us. He breathes on us. And He always speaks a better word over us. Better than our critics, better than those who want to control us, better than those who are jealous of us, and better than what we often believe about ourselves.

God sees us as we are—our true selves—and because He's not bound by the confines of time, He knows who we can be. He sees our future with as much clarity as He sees us in the present. He imprints our identity into the core of who we are. It's like a song He sings over us that is true, feels true, and brings us into the fullness of who we are when we believe His Word is true.

You have a destiny written over your life that's beautiful, powerful, and disproportionate to who you are. In other words, you can't live into the fullness of your God-given destiny without God, without His Spirit! Parts of your calling may already be clear to you, but other parts may come as a complete surprise to you. God will unveil His purposes as He prepares you to walk in them.

What's so interesting about the words spoken over me is that they proved wrong. Dead wrong. When I turned from those hurtful, cumbersome words and turned to the Lord, I knew He had a better plan for me. I learned to give more weight to His influence than theirs. I found the courage to follow Him despite my fears, my critics, and my own physical battles. With God, all your obstacles are overcomeable. (I made up that word, but let's go with it.)

You have a destiny written over your life that's beautiful, powerful, and disproportionate to who you are.

How do we tell the truth from lies and weed out the words that aren't from God? By being not only people of the Word but people of the Spirit. If you read the Word for knowledge alone, it'll likely go to your head. Scripture tells us that "while knowledge makes us feel important, it's *love* that strengthens the church" (1 Corinthians 8:1, emphasis mine). If you study the Word and forsake the idea of encountering the God who breathed that Word, you run the risk of deception, either receiving it or perpetuating it. Or both.

Jesus is all about Spirit and truth (John 4:24). If you read the Word to encounter the God of the Word, He will change you from the inside out. Not only will He give you the power to disentangle from the lies spoken over you, but He'll turn you into a warrior who helps others get free. And it'll be the *love* of God that compels you onward. It'll be the *breath* of God that infuses you with strength. And it'll be the *Word* of God that keeps you on the straight and narrow.

If we're not daily walking in the Spirit, relying on His input, and immersing ourselves in His Word, we will begin to presume upon God. We'll think we're speaking for Him when we're really speaking from our past achievements or petrified past perspectives. We—like anyone else—run the risk of misrepresenting God if we're not regularly receiving a fresh word from Him. We might be the source of those words that wound others.

Read the Scriptures (especially in the Old Testament) and notice how many people spout "As surely as the Lord lives" declarations to justify their sin and disobedience. Just because someone claims to speak for God doesn't mean they actually do. I'm especially leery of people who boldly overuse the statement "God told me to tell *you* . . ." I'm more likely to listen to a humbler approach from a trusted source that might sound something like, "I was praying for you this morning, and here's something the Lord impressed upon my heart. Take it to Him yourself. Spend time in His Word. If it resonates, keep it. If not, toss it aside for another day."

As we walk with God and spend time in His Word, we come to understand who He is and how He operates. By living our lives in response to the Holy Spirit within us, we cultivate discernment and sensitivity to His presence in and around us. We start to notice when things feel off. We feel that inner wince within us when we're off. We're wise to develop a deep dependence on God and cultivate a listening heart as a way of life.

PAUSE.

BREATHE.

PONDER.

What words were spoken over
you that still influence you?

What will you do about it?

With God's help, you can replace
the lie with the truth about who you
are and the curse with a blessing.

What beautiful, life-giving truth is
God speaking over you today?

As God's people, we strive to represent His heart to one another and to the world. But we may occasionally miss the mark, or others might. That's okay. As long as our primary source of wisdom is God, His Word, and the Holy Spirit's confirmation of His voice in our lives, we'll find ourselves on the path that God has for us.

> We're wise to develop a deep dependence on God and cultivate a listening heart as a way of life.

DAVID, A SHEPHERD KING

Sometimes we're the ones who see ourselves through a skewed lens. Sometimes, it's others who cannot see what God sees in us. That's why we must know—down to our core—what God sees when He looks at us.

When Samuel went to anoint Israel's next king, young David was out in the fields shepherding the flock. His own father thought so little of him that he didn't consider calling him home when the great prophet came to their home for a visit.

Samuel walked with God, yet even he was tempted to judge by appearance. He took one look at Jesse's son Eliab and thought, "Surely, this is the LORD's anointed!" (1 Samuel 16:6). But the Lord spoke to Samuel, "Don't judge by his appearance or height, for I have rejected him. The LORD doesn't see things the way you see them. People judge by outward appearance, but the LORD looks at the heart" (1 Samuel 16:7).

Samuel, filled with the Spirit, discerned that none of the young men standing in front of him were Israel's next king. "Are these all the sons you have?" he asked Jesse, who admitted he hadn't called them all into the house (v. 11). David's own family repeatedly dismissed him.

But God saw everything. God heard David's songs on the hillside. God infused David with the strength to kill the lion and the bear. God trained David to be a worshiper and a warrior. God knew who He was calling. And suddenly, Samuel knew too. He insisted that all these men remain standing until David arrived.

Once Samuel anointed David, the Spirit came powerfully upon David (v. 13). What did he do next? Go to the palace and sit in the king's chair? Obviously not. David went on the long, obedient, arduous journey to follow God and face his enemies, and in the process he learned to live by what God said and not by what his eyes could see.

Picture ruddy David with dirt smudges on his face, dirt under his fingernails, and passion in his heart. He was likely around fifteen years old when Samuel anointed him. His father and brothers witnessed this momentous event. Did they keep it quiet? Did they mock him out of jealousy? Did they pretend it never happened? We don't know. But it did happen. God had a better word than what any of them would have said.

David didn't take the throne overnight because that wasn't God's highest and best plan for him or Israel. He journeyed for another fifteen years before he became king. Read the Psalms to hear his passionate cries for justice, wisdom, and God's intervention. His psalms are a gift to us.

Like David's, the path to your God-given destiny is filled with enemies, obstacles, and critics. Will you set your gaze upward and trust in the one true God? Will you measure the words people speak to you against the final authority, which is God's Word? Will you remain humble and teachable while also being fierce and faithful?

God's Spirit is alive in you. His Word is alive to you! All of heaven sings over you. Access His presence. Count on His promises. And walk forward knowing that if you continually submit to God, His Word, and His ways, no demon in hell will be able to stop you.

PRAYER

Almighty God, Father in heaven,

I bow before You today. I honor You as the ultimate authority in my life! Show me the lies I picked up when life let me down. Remind me of the words spoken over me that don't align with Your purposes for me. Help me reject and renounce them, one by one.

Forgive me for my tendency to live halfheartedly for You. I want to go all in. I want my worship, my waiting, and my wondering all lifted as an offering to You. Let me hear Your song over me.

Speak a fresh word to me! Breathe on me as I read Your Word. Strengthen me to win my battles as I wait for You to fulfill Your promises. Heighten my sensitivity to Your Spirit when I'm about to believe a lie. May Your love and wisdom abound in me! Help me be a reliable messenger of healing and wholeness to this lost and broken world.

In Jesus's mighty name I pray, amen.

MOMENTS OF REFLECTION

1. Read 1 Samuel 16:1–13. Consider how David's own family dismissed him and yet God saw him. David didn't

wait for perfect circumstances to pursue God. His pain motivated his passion for God. Are your circumstances chasing you into the arms of God? How so?

2. Consider the hard parts of your story right now. What message or narrative are you tempted to believe?

3. What is the better word that God has for you? What do you sense Him saying to you in this place?

Chapter Nine

GOD, THE GREAT PHYSICIAN, HEALS ME

We've tried to become experts at not getting hurt.
We need to become experts at learning to heal.

JEFF MANION, ON
SUSIE LARSON LIVE

O Lord my God,
I cried to You for help, and You have healed me.

PSALM 30:2 AMP

The other morning, I woke up, sat on the edge of my bed, opened my hands, and prayed the same simple prayer I pray every morning:

> *O Sovereign Lord, who gives sleep to my eyes and rest to my heart, healing to my body and strength to my frame, thank You for saving me, healing me, and sealing me for the day of redemption. Thank You (by faith) for granting me the sleep I need. Fill me afresh with the wonder of Your love. Anoint me for Your service. Align my heart with Yours. Help me love what You love, do what You'd do, say what You'd say, and pray what You'd pray. Grant me the energy I need to attend to the assignments You've entrusted to me. Thank You for another day to serve You. Amen.*

The night prior, I felt like I was getting sick. Our team had just come through our fundraiser at the radio station (lots of hours on the air), and Kev and I were leaving that morning for the airport for a speaking event. Sitting on the edge of my bed, I realized I felt better than I had the night before. The scratchy throat and body aches had disappeared. The sickness didn't win. By God's grace, my healthy body had won. That was unusual for me!

I stepped out to my living room, heated my cinnamon-scented neck wrap, brewed a cup of decaf, and put my worship playlist on in my headphones. I decided to head downstairs, turn on my infrared sauna, and let it heat up during my prayer time. I wanted to sweat out any last vestiges of a cold lingering beneath the surface before Kev and I left for our event.

As soon as I walked out of my little downstairs exercise room and into the family room, God's whisper stopped me on a dime. I heard the words *Let the weak say, "I am strong." Let the poor say, "I am rich."*[1]

In a moment, I was overcome by the power of those declarations. For years, *many* years, as a young mom, God urged me to declare out loud: "Let the weak say, 'I am strong'! Let the poor say, 'I am rich'!" It always felt foolish to muster the courage to speak those words because they never felt true. Our house was falling apart. My body was falling apart. Our finances had utterly fallen apart.

But as soon as that declaration left my mouth, those words became a war cry against the Enemy of my soul. They reverberated through the air, shifted something within me, and changed the spiritual atmosphere. God was teaching me to give the Enemy notice, because my strength *continually* comes from almighty God! I learned early on that you don't have to feel well to be powerful in the Spirit. I love feeling good. More than I can possibly express. But it's not required to move mountains, shut down the Enemy, and walk powerfully on earth.

By God's grace, we can move powerfully through life, even in our weakness, because His Spirit is alive in us. *Do you know how miraculous that is?* Don't rush past that reality too quickly.

We all long to see miracles, signs, and wonders. But has it ever occurred to you that *you're a walking sign and wonder*? The Enemy knocks you down, and you get back up again. His arrows pierce your soul, and you pull them out and are quicker to armor up next time. Someone breaks your heart, and you renew your commitment to walk in love and forgive as a way of life.

> We all long to see miracles, signs, and wonders. But has it ever occurred to you that *you're a walking sign and wonder?*

You open your mouth and speak with godly wisdom, and sometimes wonder, *Where did that come from?* And just then, you know it's God. The Creator of the universe has taken up residence within you and moves powerfully through you.

Consider the number of days you've crawled out of bed in a bad mood—sad, mad, and frustrated by the weight of your burdens. And yet somehow, over the course of a few hours, God turns your day into a brilliant and beautiful one. You're not alone. You're not left to figure this out by yourself. God is with you. And that's a miracle.

But there's more. Walking from a dark room into a light room, your eyes automatically adjust to your surroundings. When you cut your finger, miraculous processes in your body activate to start the healing process. Your body produces and replaces something like 330 billion cells every day, without your input.[2] God puts breath in your lungs, life in your blood, and purpose in your steps.

No matter what the Enemy has thrown your way, you're still standing, still turning your face toward heaven, and still trusting in the name of the Lord your God.

No matter what the Enemy has thrown your way, you're still standing, still turning your face toward heaven, and still trusting in the name of the Lord your God. You're a walking miracle. Your Great Physician is always tending to you, teaching you, and guiding you along the best path for your life.

> The Lord says, "I will guide you along the best pathway
> for your life.
> I will advise you and watch over you."
>
> **PSALM 32:8**

FULL-CIRCLE MOMENTS

So there I stood, in my family room, when I realized it happened to be the exact spot eight years prior where I asked God to either kill me or heal me. In that spot I'd crumbled in a heap on the floor and told the Lord I couldn't take another step. Yet there I stood. Healthy, strong, full of faith, and rich in the goodness of God. It felt like a miracle.

I'd had a super-intense workweek with high output. We were exhausted from our fundraiser, and getting sick after such a week would not have been unusual for me.

Yet, with my feet planted in that sacred spot, I realized that my years of declaration had become a holy revelation. I looked around. My life looked nothing like it did back then. I reached out my arms to praise God as I watched the sunrise brighten the sky. It was a holy goose-bump moment. Just then, a worship song crescendoed in my ears about God's faithfulness. God was with me! Though my advances always seemed so minuscule, and my adversary always seemed unrestrained, I stood many miles and mountains away from where I had been.

My eyes beheld the sunrise. My heart skipped a beat. My feet wouldn't move. It's like God put me there to ponder my years of declaring His goodness over my hardship. Like a movie reel, I saw us back in our little blue starter house. I remembered one day when our entryway floor dropped out from underneath Kev and he stood in an entryway hole up to his armpits. It was such a picture of what our life had become. I remembered all the expensive IV bags in our fridge—Lyme treatment we couldn't afford but that I needed. There were IV bags where there should have been more food. I remembered the yellowish pee-colored house we rented when times were tough and how we felt so lost and set aside by God and friends.

Oh, the valleys we'd traveled and the hardship we'd known! But none of those painful memories stung anymore. They'd become catalysts to awe-inspiring wonder—a backdrop to God's willingness to revive and restore.

My thoughts shifted to the present. I marveled at how God had subtly (over time) yet drastically changed the landscape of our lives.

I looked around at our beautiful home, counted our amazing friends, thanked God for our precious kids and grandkids, and marveled at the kingdom purposes God had worked in and through us over the years. I stood there stunned that my body had shown the kind of resilience I hadn't seen in years.

Do I still deal daily with annoying and harassing symptoms? Yes. Do I still struggle to get a good night's sleep? Many nights, yes. Are there still giants in my land and a few sorrows in my heart? Of course. We're living behind enemy lines.

But I've gained ground. The Enemy has lost real estate in my life. He's been shoved off my land. And though I'm several years older than I was when this battle started, I'm several years stronger, wiser, and more durable than I once was. How did I get here from there? Only God. That spot in our family room, my battleground, had suddenly become my victory ground.

> You'll see . . . the wicked *won't know what hit them*;
> you'll blink, and they'll be gone;
> you'll go out looking for them, but you won't find them.
> But the humble-hearted will inherit the land;
> they will take pleasure in its peace and enjoy its
> abundance.
>
> (PSALM 37:10–11 THE VOICE)

ONE DAY, EVERYTHING CHANGED

In the heat of the Judean desert, Maya opened her eyes and realized it was already morning.[3] How long had she slept? How long until she could go back to bed? Exhaustion—not life—flowed through her

PAUSE.

BREATHE.

PONDER.

Your battleground will become
a victory ground.

You're still standing.

What blessings can you count today?

Ask God for a renewed, redemptive,
faith-filled perspective on your story.

veins, making everything an effort. Though she was barely skin and bones, her body felt heavy, too heavy. "How am I still breathing?" she wondered out loud.

Feeling the familiar dampness below, she realized she needed a change of clothes. Tired of facing the scornful looks of others, Maya took a back way to the river to wash her soiled rags. Lost in her task, she watched the blood seep into the water. She wrapped her fingers around her wet garments, squeezed the excess water, and sighed. "If only it were this easy for me to be clean, healed, and whole."

Jarred from her private ponderings, Maya heard several women shuffling toward the river, talking about the Healer who'd come to town. They talked over each other, but she heard every word. "He's a miracle worker! He healed a man of leprosy. Delivered another from demons. He's kind to the outcast and stands up to the religious leaders. We've never seen a rabbi like him!"

Maya's ears perked up. She wondered, *Could it be true? Is there really a healer in town? Not the kind who takes your money and leaves you worse off but a rabbi who cares about the people?*

Maya's thoughts drifted back over the years. When her body betrayed her and began to bleed, the people initially felt compassion, which soon shifted to suspicion. She lost her family and friends, her reputation, and her livelihood. She led a small life with few belongings and no one to advocate for her.

Maya reflected on the countless "healers" over the years who had taken her money and left her violated and humiliated. She put her hands over her abdomen and felt that familiar anxious knot balling up again. Would she ever be free? Would she ever find community again? Would there ever be a day when she didn't have to yell, "Unclean!" when people walked her way? How was this her life?

Something like hope awakened within this dear girl, and she

decided to find this Healer and see if He was everything others claimed Him to be.

Perhaps you've read this story in Scripture. I've taken a few liberties to illustrate what it may have been like for her. We don't know her name, but I chose Maya, which means "water." The Lord Jesus washed her clean.

Imagine the moment when Maya decided to press through the crowds. Never mind the social norms of the day. Forget the religious rules about her being ceremonially unclean. She had to touch Jesus's hem; she just had to grab hold of the healing that she longed for. Do you realize what kind of grit and fierce faith that took, especially after so many dashed hopes and setbacks? She's someone I can't wait to meet in heaven.

As someone who *so* looks forward to the day I'm completely symptom-free, I like to imagine what that day was like for Maya. I picture her moving from anxious fear to fierce faith as she pressed through the crowd despite the jeers and accusations from those around her.

I imagine her frail body feeling bumped and bruised by the healthy, vigorous masses competing for Jesus's attention. She was no match for them. I envision her tripping, grabbing the hem of Jesus's garment, and falling to the ground. What happened next? She could have been trampled! I picture her putting her hands to her face as she felt *life* coursing through her veins. An unfamiliar awakening overwhelmed her with fresh vitality as energy surged through her body. She knew—without a doubt—she was healed.

What happened next takes my breath away.

Jesus stopped the chaotic bustle of the crowds and focused His attention on *her*. He called her *daughter* (Luke 8:48). Up until that point, no one had claimed her. No one wanted to be associated with her. But Jesus did. That word *daughter* translates this way:

- "a daughter of God"
- "acceptable to God"
- "rejoicing in God's peculiar care and protection"[4]

Have you ever rejoiced in God's peculiar care and protection over you? He's walked with you in a very special and personal way, unique to who you are. If you paused long enough to think about it, you'd come up with one instance after another of His healing provision in your life: the times He comforted you in your grief, turned your sorrow into joy, and brought the right perspective when you needed it most. The times He helped you bounce back when you'd been knocked down. You're an absolute treasure to Him, you know?

Imagine Maya in this moment. Picture the chaos and noise of the crowds. Some were pressing in because they needed a miracle. Some were caught up in the excitement. Others were pressing through to gather evidence against Jesus.

Yet this one woman, who should have stayed home by culture's standards, showed up and went after her healing. I believe Jesus called her out not to expose her but to serve notice to her Enemy and her community that she was healed and made clean—completely, thoroughly healed and whole.

WHEN GOD FLIPS THE SCRIPT

In my book *Closer Than Your Next Breath*, I write about how God promised me that I would one day cross over from a ministry of trial to a ministry of triumph. That one day, the chronic, relentless health battles would be a thing of the past. He confirmed this word in a few profound ways. A couple of my key intercessors have been saying for a while now, "Susie, we think you've already crossed over. There's clearly a 'more' to what God is doing in and around you. We can see it! You're stronger, more resilient, and the fruit of your labor is more bountiful than we've ever seen it."

In some ways, I knew they were right. But it didn't feel completely true to me. I hated to admit it, but every time I'd go to the dentist, the doctor, or some kind of annual appointment, I'd feel that familiar surge in my nervous system that something was about to go wrong. I wasn't free, and I so wanted to be!

The other morning, a friend texted and said, "I was praying for you last night, and it occurred to me that you've had a couple of really bad experiences with doctors in your younger years. The surgeon who pulled out your chewing molars and the OB who delivered your son. Were there others?"

Like a lightning bolt, I felt the familiar anxiety surge through my body. *What in the world?* But then I sat for a moment, and the memories came flooding in . . .

I have had a handful of pretty terrible experiences at the hands of doctors. When I paused and put them all together, it's no wonder I was so easily triggered. It was as if God flipped a switch, and I could see the power grid that the Enemy had laid beneath me. Anytime my health challenges surfaced, so did the familiar anxiety of placing myself in the care of doctors.

I called my sister Karen and cried. I recalled memories of experiences that never should have happened. She listened intently, then asked the Lord what He wanted to show me in this part of my story. The very next moment, Karen started to cry. She said, "Susie, when I look at your life now, I marvel. I don't know anyone surrounded by as many good, godly doctors as you are. And they're all good friends of yours! Can you see what God has done for you?"

I gasped. She was right! Suddenly, I could see all God had redeemed in my life in Technicolor™. I realized in that moment that the lingering symptoms, fears, and weaknesses whispered continually to me: *You're still not free.* But then my sister spoke a fresh perspective to me. I zoomed out. The Lord showed me how far I'd come. By His grace, I'm not where or who I was all those years ago.

Though the Enemy continued to taunt, God built a healing infrastructure around me. I listed the doctors and friends in health care who have become precious friends and safe healers in my life:

- Dr. Troy, functional medicine
- Dr. Jill, MD and functional medicine
- Dr. Jimmy, internist and general medicine
- Dr. Tom, trauma surgeon
- Dr. Stefan, brain/spine neurosurgeon
- Dr. Lee, brain/spine surgeon and mind-renewal expert
- Dr. George, MD and pain specialist
- Dr. Rob, soul-care expert
- Tiffani, ICU nurse
- Jodi, hospice nurse
- Tami, massage therapist (who prays over me during my massage)
- Amie, physical therapist (brilliant woman of God who prays over me while she works)
- Jamie, integrative nutrition, health coach

Thank the Lord for the memories that surface to help us remember where we were. Thank Him for the moments of truth that reveal where we *actually* are! One moment in God's presence changes everything. And as we journey with God, we will continually need upgrades and updates in our perspective.

If we pay attention to God's leadership in our lives, He will show us how He will turn for good what the Enemy meant for evil, and often, for the saving of many lives (Genesis 50:20). He transforms our pain into a testimony for the many who are influenced by our lives.

> One moment in God's presence changes everything.

Though God is not the author of your hardship, He is the King over all. He can and will use every detail—from the hard and the painful to the beautiful—to write your masterful story. One that overwhelms you and that brings Him glory.

In a matter of moments, God flipped the switch so I could see the power grid the Enemy had been using against me; then He flipped the script and showed me that I am no longer in the place I once was. Regarding health care, yes, there was a pattern of theft in my younger years. But that was *then,* and this is now.

Part of my calling is to help others heal, whatever that looks like. I often cover health topics on my show, *Susie Larson Live.* And whether on the air, at speaking events, or in a private setting, I pray for miracles for others regularly. If we can assist others with their medical bills, we do that too. Although the Enemy laid a foundation of fear in my early years, God established a foundation of faithfulness, protection, and provision as He healed me.

My pain served as a catalyst for my calling to help others. It's the same with you. Where the Enemy has struck you the hardest is where you'll see God's faithful, peculiar protection and provision. From that place, your calling will spring forth.

Make space for healing. Make space for Jesus. Slow down and listen for His gentle whisper. Listen to your body. When you drive it too hard, it'll tell you. When you rush past mourning, it'll remind

Make space for healing. Make space for Jesus.

you. When you ignore old memories, they'll resurface. God has written His laws in nature, science, and even in our bodies. His ways are higher than our ways (Isaiah 55:8–9). He wants us to participate with Him in our healing process. Make space for Jesus. Make space to heal. Dr. Saundra Dalton-Smith writes:

> Picture yourself surrounded by nature's beauty, the gentle caress of a breeze, the warmth of the sun on your skin—reminders of the Creator's intimate presence in every fiber of your being. Through practices of self-care—restful sleep, nourishing meals, mindful movement—we can honor our bodies and invite God's healing.[5]

I encourage you to get outside as often as you can. Look up at the sky, take a deep breath, and marvel at God's handiwork. We're in such good hands. But your body needs to know those truths. So, slow down, enjoy God's beauty, breathe deeply, create some margin in your schedule, and truly believe that God wants to breathe fresh life in and through you.

Until you see Jesus face-to-face, you will be on a healing journey. God loves intimacy and responds to faith. Count on Him to lead you on the path of life. Invite Him to show you perspectives or beliefs that hold you captive. Dare to be like Maya, discontent to be just one of the many in the crowd. She wanted her own experience with God, and she got one. Her faith grabbed Jesus's attention and changed her story.

The God of Angel Armies is also your Great Physician. He's the One who heals. He's the One who redeems. He's the One who rescues.

And He's the One who takes our broken selves and our broken stories and makes something beautiful out of all of it.

> I waited patiently for the Lord to help me,
> and he turned to me and heard my cry.
> He lifted me out of the pit of despair,
> out of the mud and the mire.
> He set my feet on solid ground
> and steadied me as I walked along.
> He has given me a new song to sing,
> a hymn of praise to our God.
> Many will see what he has done and be amazed.
> They will put their trust in the Lord.
>
> (PSALM 40:1-3)

PRAYER

Precious Jesus,

You've already healed so much in my life. Thank You!

Help me not to miss Your wonder-working power in my story. Bring to remembrance the countless ways You've rescued, redeemed, and restored me. Show me the places in my soul and story that still need Your healing power.

Help me never to settle for less than Your best for me! Awaken my heart to live by faith, to look for Your goodness, and to count on Your healing power in my life. Healing and saving, redeeming and restoring . . . that's who You are; that's what You do. Thank You for being so good and so involved in my story.

I declare over my life: I am healing! God is mightily at work in me, redeeming my story for His glory! I receive it, believe it, and walk in it!

In Jesus's name I pray, amen.

MOMENTS OF REFLECTION

1. Read "Maya's" story in Mark 5:24–34 and prayerfully ask God what parts of her story He wants to highlight to you. Write down your thoughts.

2. What in you still needs healing? Talk to God about it.

3. Imagine the day when Jesus holds your face in His hands and says to you, "My precious one, your suffering is over." Wow. Thank God now because that day is coming.

Chapter Ten

GOD DELIVERS ME FROM ALL MY FEARS

If you've ever experienced the comfort of God, or the love of God, that was heaven coming to you here on earth.

JOHN ELDREDGE, *RESILIENT*

I sought (inquired of) the Lord and required Him [of necessity and on the authority of His Word], and He heard me, and delivered me from all my fears.

PSALM 34:4 AMPC

Fear has been an unwelcome traveling companion my whole life. I'm not fearless, but I'm not the fearful person I once was. My freedom has come in layers. Every time I experience something of God's goodness, provision, or protection, the threat response within me diminishes, and the good moments eclipse the painful ones. Even so, I've got a ways to go. But whenever I'm in a position to face my fears or I hear of how God came through for someone else, I'm inspired to give more weight to God's promises than I do my fears. He's always working, always inviting us to new depths of trust in Him.

He's always working, always inviting us to new depths of trust in Him.

Recently, I was invited to speak on a remote island in the Bahamas. Initially I was convinced it was a scam and almost dismissed it. The inquiry didn't come through our website like most invitations do. But to my surprise, it turned out to be a legitimate invitation.

My initial instinctive response was *no*. Kev investigated potential flights and found out we'd have to wake up at 3:00 a.m. for an early departure, and we wouldn't get back home until midnight a few days later. Sleep has been a significant issue for me, so that alone made me hesitate. Additionally, there was the risk of mold on a remote tropical island with no hospitals or hotels. I've mentioned how mold affects me in devastating ways, neurologically and cognitively. After two flights and a ferry ride, I'd be stranded if there were no clean places to stay. Everything in *me* wanted to stay home. I knew I needed to take this decision to the Lord and seek His counsel.

INQUIRING OF THE LORD

There are plenty of examples of people in Scripture who inquired of the Lord and made righteous choices, or who went ahead without seeking Him first, only to suffer the consequences. There are three ways to respond to every and any situation in which we find ourselves: (1) Listen to the Enemy, (2) think to ourselves, or (3) inquire of the Lord.[1]

WHEN WE LISTEN TO THE ENEMY

Our brains and bodies hold on to trauma and fear more instinctively than we hold on to redemption and love. That's why the Enemy's weapon of fear is so effective. He keeps a good record of our fears. When opportunities and even adventures arise, the spirit of fear jumps in our way and convinces us to turn back. When we're hurting, broken, or just tired and weary, the Enemy wastes no time feeding us worst-case scenarios. He wants us to imagine (and fear) a future that God is not in. But he doesn't get to do that. For the Christ follower, no such scenario exists.

There's no future moment for the believer that God is not in. And the devil knows it. He's the one who faces his whole future apart from God. He doesn't get to enjoy intimacy with God. He'll never again be on the winning side. He can destroy things, but he can't rebuild them. He'll never have what we have in Jesus. He threatens us because we're a threat to him.

Whatever you're afraid of, know this: There's life, peace, adventure, and a blessing on the other side of that fear. Listening to the Enemy will always lead us further into captivity. Listening to and following Jesus will always lead you to deeper places of freedom and redemption. You'll never experience the best of what God has for you if your fears mean more to you than God's love. It's His voice, His character, and His promise that guard and guide you. Part of becoming who God created you to be involves trusting God with your fears.

WHEN WE THINK TO OURSELVES

David was afraid. Saul relentlessly pursued David, wanting him dead. He didn't fight fairly. Jealousy, greed, fear, and self-preservation fueled his paranoia. David fought as honorably as he could. But being hunted by someone you faithfully served and who desires your death can take a toll on anyone. When we're worn from battle, we naturally rely on our own understanding. Scripture says, "David *thought to himself*, 'Saul will catch me some day. The best thing I can do is to escape to the land of the Philistines. Then Saul will give up looking for me in Israel. That way I will escape from Saul'" (1 Samuel 27:1 ERV, emphasis mine).

> You'll never experience the best of what God has for you if your fears mean more to you than God's love.

How many fear-based decisions do we make because we're *thinking to ourselves* about ourselves? Left to ourselves, we cycle through our fearful history and self-preserving tactics and try to eke out some certainty and control over our story. But it never works in the long term. We miss out on so much when we make decisions based on past experiences, unprocessed fears, and our skewed, limited perspective. In his book *Living Fearless*, Jamie Winship writes:

> Trusting God in his true identity of shepherd-poet-warrior-king, David is invincible. When he switches to *asking himself for advice*, he becomes fearful and decides to run. Self-protection and self-preservation are always the strategy of a fearful person and an indicator of the false self taking charge.[2]

When we think to ourselves, we mostly think about ourselves. We miss out on God's precious, faith-filled, life-giving, history-making input, which is the *very thing* that transforms us as we go. We only know in part. And what we do know is partial and incomplete. God sees it all, knows everything, and lavishes more love on us than our bodies can contain! He loves us most and knows us best. We need Him every moment of every hour. When we inquire of the Lord, we take God-inspired risks, we lay down our fears and trust His love, and we avoid much collateral damage from the Enemy.

> *The shepherds of my people have lost their senses.*
> They no longer seek wisdom from the LORD.
> Therefore, they fail completely,
> and their flocks are scattered.
>
> (JEREMIAH 10:21, EMPHASIS MINE)

WHEN WE INQUIRE OF THE LORD

When we turn away from the Enemy's voice and acknowledge that we cannot fully trust our own emotional processing, we can look upward to Jesus's face and finally see and hear clearly. Only God's voice can thunder through the chaos, overwhelm the fear, and bring peace where there is none. Only God can bring clarity out of confusion and fierce faith where there once was fear. God can speak to us about a future we cannot, from this place, imagine. Inquiring of the Lord can keep us out of trouble and lead us into mountain-moving, life-changing experiences.

After inquiring of the Lord, my husband and I sensed the call to say yes to the Bahamas invitation. I was taking all kinds of risks health-wise (and when those risks backfire, it can take me weeks to recover). But we felt the Lord's peace and even an urging to go with expectant hearts.

I don't have words to describe what we experienced when we said yes to God. From getting up in the middle of the night to catch the plane to taking two flights and a ferry boat to our destination, we felt encircled by God's love and surrounded by His care. I was so deeply dependent on God for every step, and I experienced more intimacy with Him than I had in weeks. If you're healthy and resilient, I'm so happy for you! If you struggle with your health, you know these disruptions to your rhythms can be overwhelming. But this time, all Kev and I experienced was God's grace and supernatural resilience.

God created an instant bond with our new friends Erica and Dave, Pastor Brooks, and his wonderful wife, Rachael. It felt like meeting old friends for the first time. They welcomed us with open arms and cared for us exceptionally well. I spoke about identity, unprocessed grief, and trusting God for new beginnings. Women flocked to the altar, bravely trusting God with their fears and heartbreaks. I sensed God's overwhelming love for these women and stood in awe of the kingdom life on this remote island.

The Lord also blessed us with sacred, restful moments. We walked along the beach, swam in the clear, turquoise waters, and marveled at the beauty around us. I never once felt unsafe. I felt at home with God. I sensed His presence.

Instead of scanning my surroundings for hints of danger, I reveled in God's goodness, knowing He had led me to this place. I saw people as image bearers—people with stories that I wanted to hear. My thoughts were on their needs, not on my safety or my symptoms.

When you're in fear, you're bracing for impact and instinctively self-protecting, which makes you miss all the God-given opportunities around you and all the God appointments assigned to you. Oh, how I longed for a braver soul so I could continue giving God bigger yeses.

On the ferry ride back to shore after a beautiful weekend of ministry, Rachael (Pastor Brooks's wife) and I sat on a bench, and I asked her more about her story. She shared that she never wanted to live on a remote island. She is from the States and loves modern conveniences just like I do. But God called them there, to a different remote island at that time. She talked about the difficult years of dealing with their trauma and hardships. Fear, anxiety, and life's stresses left them in a tough place.

Over a decade ago, they moved to Nassau, the capital of the Bahamas, to assist Brooks's mom. Rachael revealed that their marriage was strained; they had a lot of hurt to address, and they were merely getting by. She cried out to God morning, noon, and night. She pleaded with Him to show Himself strong on her behalf.

One day, Rachael picked up her young daughters from school. One of her daughters had a friend with her for a sleepover. It was a beautiful day, but the sky rumbled with thunder. A storm was brewing, in more ways than one. Rachael pulled into the driveway as the rain began to fall. She said, "Girls, I'm going to get you into the front door, and then I'll come back for your backpacks."

As she walked back out of her front door and toward her car, she noticed a large man approaching her aggressively, with a gun concealed under his shirt. Rachael swallowed hard, realizing she was in trouble. He grabbed her arm and shoved her through her front door. With his gun aimed at her, he demanded, "Lock us in. Lock that door." Spouting a string of expletives, he shouted, "Give me the cash! Where's the [blankety-blank] cash?"

She knew she needed to be strong for her girls, so she stood her ground and said, "I have no cash! Please leave!" He screamed at her and then at the girls, ordering the girls to lie face down and not look up. He continued to demand money, which she did not have.

The burglar then stepped back, scanned her body up and down and said, "Take me to your bedroom." She prayed and asked God for strength and protection. They walked down the hall to the bedroom, and the burglar turned toward her. Again, he demanded cash, and she told him she had no money.

As she stood there, wondering if the unthinkable was about to happen, she heard God's voice as clear as day. The Lord thundered in her spirit, *Rachael, I am the Good Shepherd. My sheep know My voice, and they follow Me. The thief comes to steal, kill, and destroy, but I have come to give you life, and life to the full. He cannot snatch you out of My hand!*

Rachael saw that passage from John 10 in real time, in real life. She saw how ruthless our Enemy can be, and yet, in that moment, she sensed how present God truly was.

Rachael said, "After that, there was like a force field around me. The Holy Spirit was in the room with me. The Enemy was being held back by the Good Shepherd's mighty hand. It was like a snap in a moment of time. I remembered I had my wedding rings, a watch, and a purse. I gave him all those things and asked him to please leave. And just like that, he said, 'Walk me to the door.' Then he left." They found out later that this man was not only a burglar but a rapist too.

Later that night, Rachael snuggled with Brooks and retold the part of the story where the Good Shepherd saved her and delivered her from her fears. Brooks pulled her close and apologized for not putting a hedge of protection around her as her husband. He'd been distracted and stressed, and their marriage had been strained and difficult. He should have more fervently prayed for his family's protection on a regular basis. It was in that moment that God turned everything around.

Rachael and Brooks both understood that, by themselves, they were no match for their Enemy. He fights dirty. But with God, anything is possible (Matthew 19:26). God used an overplayed Enemy attack to position them for redemption and freedom. They started to rebuild their marriage with the help and guidance of the Holy Spirit. God healed them in more ways than one.

If you could see them now, you'd stand amazed. They love each other deeply. They have a thriving ministry on this beautiful island. The poor hear the good news. The captives are being set free. People are coming to Christ and seeing their lives transformed. One woman on the island told me about a season of unbearable loss. But then she looked up at me with sparkling eyes and said, "If I knew then what I know now . . . I can't believe how God has restored me!"

One life at a time, stories are changing on that island because Rachael and Brooks didn't run away out of fear. They ran toward God and followed His lead. They deeply, intimately trust Him and rely on Him. And they're trusting their Good Shepherd to lead them every step of the way.

Fear didn't get to have the last say in their story, and it won't have the last say in mine. Running headlong into your fears isn't wise. But following the Good Shepherd wherever He leads is life! If He leads you to face your fears, it's because there's something beautiful waiting for you on the other side.

> "Come to me with your ears wide open.
> Listen, and you will find life.

PAUSE.

BREATHE.

PONDER.

Are you listening to the Enemy
regarding that thing you fear?

Thinking to yourself?

Or inquiring of the Lord?

> I will make an everlasting covenant with you.
> I will give you all the unfailing love I promised to
> David."
>
> (ISAIAH 55:3)

GET YOUR HOPES UP!

Of all the scary things in this world that might cause us fear, one sneaks under our radar. Many of us fear to hope. What do we do if we fear getting our hopes up, lest they be dashed? The Bible tells us.

> One day Elisha went to the town of Shunem. A wealthy woman lived there, and she urged him to come to her home for a meal. After that, whenever he passed that way, he would stop there for something to eat.
>
> She said to her husband, "I am sure this man who stops in from time to time is a holy man of God. Let's build a small room for him on the roof and furnish it with a bed, a table, a chair, and a lamp. Then he will have a place to stay whenever he comes by."
>
> One day Elisha returned to Shunem, and he went up to this upper room to rest. He said to his servant Gehazi, "Tell the woman from Shunem I want to speak to her." When she appeared, Elisha said to Gehazi, "Tell her, 'We appreciate the kind concern you have shown us. What can we do for you? Can we put in a good word for you to the king or to the commander of the army?'"
>
> "No," she replied, "my family takes good care of me."
>
> Later Elisha asked Gehazi, "What can we do for her?"
>
> Gehazi replied, "She doesn't have a son, and her husband is an old man."

"Call her back again," Elisha told him. When the woman returned, Elisha said to her as she stood in the doorway, "Next year at this time you will be holding a son in your arms!"

"No, my lord!" she cried. "O man of God, don't deceive me and get my hopes up like that."

But sure enough, the woman soon became pregnant. And at that time the following year, she had a son, just as Elisha had said.

(2 KINGS 4:8–17)

When Elisha first asked this woman if there was anything he could do for her, she essentially replied, "No. I'm good!" Coming from a well-to-do home, she felt content. But when Elisha summoned her again and told her she would have a baby by this time next year, she forcefully blurted, "*No,* O man of God! Don't deceive me and get my hopes up like that!"

Elisha had hit a nerve, touching on a topic that was too painful for her to discuss. This dear woman knew Elisha was a prophet. Yet when he spoke to her about her buried dreams, she strongly reacted in fear with a big, fat *no!* She had suffered so much trauma around infertility that she saw Elisha incorrectly. She accused him of deceiving her and getting her hopes up. Ever been there?

When you're in fear and in denial of your deepest desires, you'll wrongly assess people and circumstances. When you're stuffing down what you want the most, your emotions and perspectives will often skew toward self-protection. We've all been there and done that, but we're not made to live that way.

Sometimes our *no* bubbles up because of fear. Other times, because of control. It's one thing to have preferences about how you want your story to go. It's another to insist on controlling your story because you think your way is better than God's. Most times, our control is fueled by our fear.

Does your fear compel you to take control of your life because God hasn't come through for you yet? If that's you, I wish I could wrap you in an embrace and pray a prayer of healing and redemption over you. I've been there too, too many times. But God, in His patience, continually guides me to places of surrender. I always find peace when I trust Him more than I trust myself.

Other times, it's not that we think our way is better than God's, but rather, we've resigned ourselves to our sorrow and hopelessness because there's not a fiber in our being that dares to hope. Maybe survival has become normal for you. Again, I *so* feel for you. And I say this with all my heart: *God is tender with your pain and gentle with your weakness. He's tending to you even now.*

> "A broken reed He will not break [off]
> And a dimly burning wick He will not extinguish
>   [He will not harm those who are weak and
>   suffering];
> He will faithfully bring forth justice."
>
> (ISAIAH 42:3 AMP)

Walking with God, facing fears, and resurrecting buried dreams require humility, vulnerability, and courage. But oh, what awaits us on the other side!

In my book *Waking Up to the Goodness of God*, I write about my son Jake, who found himself in a similar place. After seven long years of heartbreaking infertility with his dear wife, he was terrified to get his hopes up. Hope felt too costly. Too expensive. When they decided to try the IVF process again, I told him I'd pray they would accelerate the paperwork.

In that moment, Jake grabbed my arm and gently scolded me. He said, "Mom! Don't pray that for me. That's not what I want. That's not helpful right now. I don't need this process to speed up. I need my heart to heal. Our hopes have been dashed so many times; I need a heart that has space for hope. I'm terrified right now. Pray that I can make space for hope."[3] My eyes welled with tears. He was right.

God is tender with your pain and gentle with your weakness. He's tending to you even now.

Allow me to ask you a few questions:

- Can you make space for hope?
- Is there a pain in your heart, a dashed dream that hurts so badly that you won't talk to God about it?
- Have you made determinations about your life that exclude the possibility of a miracle—that don't account for the miraculous, sovereign power of almighty God?

Sometimes it's easier to bury our dreams and allow our fears to dictate our lives. It may be easier, but it's not better. God has so much life yet for you to live! He has so much goodness yet to impart! Your best days are not behind you. They're ahead of you!

But when fear and unresolved grief take up residence in your heart, you begin to see and assess circumstances incorrectly. Great is the temptation to self-sabotage and put yourself out of your misery. You don't dare to hope because you don't want to hurt, so you decide for yourself what God will or will not do for you. Let me ask again: *Can you make space for hope?*

Don't put a period at the end of a sentence that God is still writing!

- When we say no to God, we say yes to the Enemy.
- When we shut the door on God, we open the door to the Enemy.
- When we say no to God, some of our story is diminished.
- When we say no to the Enemy, some of his plans are demolished!

Sometimes it's easier to bury our dreams and allow our fears to dictate our lives. It may be easier, but it's not better. God has so much life yet for you to live!

The Enemy is the one who should be hearing our noes!

You may feel right now that God is holding out on you. But maybe, could it be, that you're holding out on Him? Have you put conditions on your story? Have you drawn boundary lines with God? Maybe it's time to give all your hang-ups, fears, and control to the One who made you and loves you deeply. He's better than you know and safer than you can imagine.

After seven years of painful setbacks and heartbreaks, God gave my son Jake and Lizzie a baby girl: Juniper Grace. She's pure joy and a treasured gift from God. They're overwhelmed by God's goodness. She was worth the wait.

Now, let me say this: Not every story (in this life) ties up in a nice, tidy bow. *But* God has a 100 percent success rate in redeeming stories!

If you're willing to make space for hope, if you're ready to trust Him, He will move, redeem, and restore in ways that take your breath away.

What if you dared to put your fears on the altar? What if you put your control on the altar? What if you humbly opened your hands and prayed, *God, I will confidently trust You to care for me. You get to decide how this story goes. You are the God who delivers me from all my fears.*

Yes, we encounter trouble in this life—Jesus promised as much (John 16:33). But when we bring Jesus into the center of it all, when we allow His perfect love to cast out fear, we will live perpetually surprised by His goodness, amazed by His power, and transformed by His love.

God wants us to go from strength to strength, glory to glory, shining ever brighter until the full light of day. This requires a few things from us: Trust. Courage. Surrender. Faith. And an intimate walk with almighty God, who establishes His best purposes for us every moment of every day.

PRAYER

Precious Father,

Thank You for loving me like You do. Thank You for Your patience with me. Fill me afresh with Your Holy Spirit. Baptize me anew in Your perfect love. Awaken me to new levels of faith, courage, and clarity.

Are there places in my story that I'm still trying to control? Show me, Lord! Is fear having the last say? Lead me, Lord. I surrender my whole life to You. With all my heart, I believe that on the other side of my fears is life abundant.

You have more for me, I know it! I want to live my life

so focused on You, so filled with Your Spirit, that I will go where You send me and minister in love, power, and grace.

I'm done with self-preservation. I want to live with kingdom passion and Calvary love. Only You, Lord, can make that a reality.

Have Your way in me.

In Jesus's name I pray, amen.

MOMENTS OF REFLECTION

1. Read 2 Kings 4:8–17 and notice how the Shunammite woman went from "No, I'm good!" to "No! Don't deceive me like that! Don't get my hopes up!" Is there an area of loss or disappointment in your life that triggers you? Write down your thoughts.

2. Are you willing to start a conversation with God about this part of your story? If so, write out your prayer and then sit and listen for a while.

3. What is God asking of you? What do you sense He wants you to do?

Conclusion

IDENTITY DECLARATION

Stay the course, my friend. You're almost home! The cloud of witnesses is cheering you on (Hebrews 12:1)! I'm cheering for you too. Every move you make, prompted by faith, hope, and love, is noted in heaven for a future reward. Know this: As a child of God, bought by the precious blood of the Lamb, your name is written in the Book of Life (Revelation 20:15). When you stand before the God of heaven, His kind and compassionate eyes will melt your heart. When He lovingly rewards you for your suffering, offerings, obedience, and perseverance, your knees will buckle right out from under you. You'll cry tears of joy and know that your troubles are finally over.

Whatever is breaking your heart right now, Jesus will soon heal it. Whatever burden you're carrying right now, Jesus will soon lift it. Though you may not always see the evidence or the fruit in the moment, your abiding life changes things. Because you've partnered with the Almighty, your journey is transforming you, your trust is strengthening you, and your faith is moving your mountains.

We are living in the times of the now and the not yet. For now,

> You're not only overcoming, you're *becoming* . . . everything God intended for you to be.

we continually possess His promises, enjoy His presence, and trust His provision until we see Him face-to-face.

Jesus is coming soon! You were called and created for far more than your precious mind could ever comprehend. May you become increasingly aware of the Holy Spirit's presence. May your ability to know His love grow exponentially in the days ahead.

May you believe wholeheartedly that God is writing a magnificent story with your life, and that He made you to live free, with purpose. You're not only overcoming, you're *becoming* . . . everything God intended for you to be.

Because of Jesus, you were made for more! You and I have scratched the surface of what He's made available to us. As you walk intimately with God and trust His love, you will *grow* as you go. Imagine a more healed, whole, free *you*! Picture yourself following and serving Jesus with greater boldness and clarity. Declare these truths over your life until you believe them in your soul.

I will live loved!	God owes me nothing but gives me everything.
God gives me purpose and power.	God always speaks a better word.
God fills me with unwavering faith.	God, the Great Physician, heals me.
God cultivates good fruit in me.	God delivers me from all my fears.
God rescues and restores me.	God has made me for more.
God strengthens me and moves my mountains.	

PRAYER

Almighty, infinite Father,

I praise Your name! I bow humbly before You and honor You with my whole life!

You have called me out of darkness and into Your marvelous light. Help me live as one who is spoken for. Show me the areas in my life that make me vulnerable to enemy attacks. Reveal to me the places that need godly and wise reinforcement. When I fear You, I need not fear anything else.

You are the High King of heaven, and I am in good hands. My soul rejoices, and I rest secure in Your love. Pour out Your Spirit afresh on me. Help me to cultivate a lifestyle of intimacy with You. Help me to earnestly forgive in every situation. Help me to live the free, healed, whole life that Jesus died for. Show me how to help others find freedom.

Mark my life with Your glory, power, and redemptive purposes. I want every step I take on earth to reflect the promises and purposes of heaven. Here I am, Lord. Work mightily in and through me.

In Jesus's name I pray, amen.

MOMENTS OF REFLECTION

Read Hebrews 12 and notice how the passage first invites you to take inventory, and then to remain teachable when God corrects you, and then to reflect on the majesty of almighty God. What most stands out to you in this chapter?

How might you cultivate greater intimacy in your walk with God?

What does obedience look like for you in this season of life?

PERSONAL STUDY QUESTIONS

CHAPTER ONE: LIVING LOVED

1. Read 1 Samuel 10. Notice that Saul hid behind the baggage when he was supposed to rise up and be counted. Prayerfully ponder a time when you've done the same. Why were you afraid? What's the cost of such fear?

2. Read 2 Timothy 1:7. Ponder the fact that fear (when it harasses, threatens, and intimidates) is a spirit, and it's not from God. Spend some time with this passage and ask God to help you understand the power, love, and sound mind He has given you.

3. Read 1 John 4:18. The word "perfect" in this passage means matured, or established. In other words, when you mature and are more established in the love God has for you, it will be more intuitive to reject fear. Write out a prayer asking God to help you to grow in the knowledge of His love

and to learn to live loved like it's the most important thing about you!

CHAPTER TWO: GOD GIVES ME PURPOSE AND POWER

1. Read Matthew 16:21–23. Reflect on how and why Peter's response might have been a stumbling block for Jesus. Write about a time when someone's fleshly response became a stumbling block for you (such as a toxic compassion that justified destructive sin or a fear-based reaction that hindered you from acting in faith). How did that affect you?

2. Read Matthew 16:24–27. Reflect on how self-preservation robs us of the rewards of our faith. As God's redeemed children, He rewards everything driven by our faith, hope, and love. God rewards our obedience and trust. He rewards our heart-felt kindness and forgiveness. He rewards our generosity and persistent prayers. In what ways does self-preservation hinder us? How has it prevented you from receiving something God wanted to do for you or through you? Take time to reflect on these questions and jot down your thoughts.

3. Read 1 Peter 2:1–10 and compare the references to sin with the calling and privilege of belonging to Jesus. Consider how easy it is to drift into sin and to forget who we really are in Christ Jesus. Write your reflections down.

CHAPTER THREE: GOD FILLS ME WITH UNWAVERING FAITH

1. Read Romans 4:17 and ask God what He wants to bring back to life in your life and what He wants to call into existence that doesn't exist (that you know of) yet.

2. Read Matthew 25:1–13 and consider the wise bridesmaids and the foolish ones. The foolish bridesmaids presumed upon God. They figured they could postpone their intimacy with Him for another day. God invites us to so much more than the world has to offer. Are there any time-wasters or distractions keeping you from a deeper, more purposeful pursuit of God? What are they, and how could you begin to let go of them?

3. Read Psalm 23:5–6 and visualize God doing exactly this for you! Imagine Him setting a royal table in the midst of your battlefield. Picture Him—dressed in royal attire—holding a flask over your head and anointing you, signifying that you have His favor and that He has empowered you. This is true, you know. If you walk in the fear of the Lord, you will find Him faithful in your battle. How aware are you of this reality in your current circumstances? How might more awareness of this change your response to the challenges you're going through right now? Write down your thoughts.

4. Read Psalm 92 and take your time. Personalize this passage. Meditate on it until it becomes your own. When you get to

verse 10, read the rest of the verses out loud—shout them out! Make them a faith declaration! He has made you as strong as an ox and anointed you with fine oil! Receive it. Believe it!

CHAPTER FOUR: GOD CULTIVATES GOOD FRUIT IN ME

1. Why do you suppose God favored Joseph?

2. Read Genesis 39:6–23 and, once again, observe the injustice Joseph endured and the favor he experienced. Write down some tangible examples of how God's favor played out in Joseph's life.

3. Imagine how you would feel if you were accused and convicted of a crime you didn't commit. Yet somehow, Joseph continued to trust God with his life. What attitudes might Joseph have been tempted to embrace? How do you think he worked through them? How do you return to a place of peace and trust when you've been treated unfairly?

4. Joseph's entire story is worth reading, but for the sake of time, fast-forward to Genesis 45. Read the entire chapter, then return to verses 5–7. Reflect on that passage for a while. Joseph didn't arrive at this point overnight; he nurtured a relationship with God that enabled him to see his brothers with redemptive eyes. Remarkable. Write down your thoughts.

CHAPTER FIVE: GOD RESCUES AND RESTORES ME

1. Read Joshua 2:8–11 and consider Rahab's faith. God's power had affected her. First Corinthians 4:20 tells us that "the kingdom of God is not a matter of talk but of power" (NIV). What stories of God's power have shaped your faith (from Scripture, saints of old, or from your life experiences)? Write down your thoughts.

2. Read Joshua 2:12–21 and note two things: Rahab's concern for her family and the symbolic red cord that represents Passover. Which family members or loved ones are you worried about? Reflect on how Scripture foretold the coming Messiah. We live in new covenant times, and there's more love and power in Jesus's blood than there is sin in the hearts of your loved ones. Keep praying and keep believing. God hears you, and He's moving. Write down a prayer of faith for your loved ones.

3. Read Psalm 18 and stand in awe of how God hears our prayers, rescues us, and sets our feet on solid ground. Write down the passages in this psalm that mean the most to you right now.

4. Read Matthew 1:5 and 1:17, and notice how Rahab is included in the genealogy of Christ. Thank Him for providing a way for *you*.

CHAPTER SIX: GOD STRENGTHENS ME AND MOVES MY MOUNTAINS

1. Read Joshua 3:5 and notice how Joshua charged the people to consecrate themselves because God was about to do something

extraordinary. Read the full chapter. Consider the miracle. Consider why God wanted their hearts prepared. Write down your thoughts.

2. Read Joshua 5:13–15 and observe how God prepared Joshua for his next battle. God never humiliates His children; however, He does humble us. Reflect on a moment when God humbled you before you were used greatly or before facing a challenge. In hindsight, do you see how He is watching out for you?

3. Read Joshua 7:1–13 and remember, the Israelites had just won a sound victory. And then they experienced a humbling defeat. What happened? Write down your thoughts.

4. Reread verse 13 and ask the Lord to show you if there's any compromise in your camp, anything He wants you to deal with. Consider your Enemy; consider your God. Fear the Lord and do what He says. Your Enemy will not be able to stand against you.

CHAPTER SEVEN: GOD OWES ME NOTHING BUT GIVES ME EVERYTHING

1. Read Job 19:25–27 and consider Job's declaration amid intense suffering. Write down what you know about God—no matter what you're going through. What do you know to be true about Him?

2. Read 1 Corinthians 4:1–5 and notice Paul's charge not to prematurely judge or assess things before the right time. And

when's the right time? When Christ returns. What types of situations are you most tempted to judge? Be honest. Ask God for a biblical perspective.

3. Read 1 Peter 5:6–11 and break down this passage into segments: your actions and God's promises. Ponder what you've unpacked and write down your thoughts.

4. Read Romans 8:26–39 and reflect on how the Holy Spirit intercedes for you, praying on your behalf when you don't know how to pray for yourself. Write out your thoughts on this magnificent passage. Take at least two or three paragraphs to contemplate the wonder of what God offers here. Write your thoughts, too, on how earthly suffering never interrupts the flow of God's love toward us.

CHAPTER EIGHT: GOD ALWAYS SPEAKS A BETTER WORD

1. In this chapter we explore David's life, but let's dig in and see what we can learn from Saul's mistakes because it was Saul's sins that disqualified him. Just because he was in a position of power didn't mean he spoke accurately. In fact, most times, he misrepresented God. Read 1 Samuel 13:13–14 and consider how Saul's actions blocked God's goodness toward him. Read verses 1–14 and notice how and why Saul disobeyed God. Write down your thoughts.

2. Read 1 Samuel 20 (the whole chapter). Notice verses 30–33

and marvel at Saul's behavior toward his own son. When Saul was anointed king, the Spirit of God fell upon him. But over time, Saul made it all about him and operated in the flesh. This moment was beyond a fleshly moment; a demonic force influenced Saul. Someone once asked, "How much can God bless you before you make it about you?" Ponder our tendency to make life too much about us. Write out your thoughts and maybe a prayer.

3. Notice that despite Jonathan's traumatic experience with his father, he maintained honor and integrity. He feared God enough to see how God was moving in Israel. What about Jonathan's responses to David and Saul most stands out to you?

4. There's a point in Saul's story where he was so raving mad that he sent men to kill David. Yet, instead of killing David, the men encountered the Spirit of God, and they began to prophesy! Read 1 Samuel 19:18–24 and consider how, although the Enemy intends evil, God's purposes prevail. Write down your thoughts about this story.

5. Read 1 Samuel 24 and notice how David's men attempted to speak for God ("Today, the LORD is telling you . . ."). But they were wrong. David was a man of deep conviction. Personalize this story. Do you walk closely enough with the Lord that if even your closest friends tell you what they think God is saying, you're able to discern His voice for yourself? Write down your thoughts.

CHAPTER NINE: GOD, THE GREAT PHYSICIAN, HEALS ME

1. Read Mark 5:35–43 and notice that Jesus—on His way to heal Jairus's daughter—had time for the woman whom society had cast aside. But also note that because Jesus took the time to help "Maya," Jairus's daughter died. Reflect on God's mysterious ways regarding healing. Write down your thoughts.

2. Read Psalm 40:1–3 and write a personalized application for these verses. In what ways have you waited on God, and how has He rescued you? Who are the "many" who see you and hear you and put their trust in the Lord because of God's involvement in your life?

3. Read Psalm 103:1–5 and write down personal examples of some ways God has fulfilled these six promises in your life.

4. Read Isaiah 40:26–31 and do a heart check. Has your perspective drifted to the mindset that God doesn't see or care? Look at the passage again and consider how He responds to those who actively engage with Him, who wait on Him with a holy expectancy (not just passively biding their time).

CHAPTER TEN: GOD DELIVERS ME FROM ALL MY FEARS

1. Have you ever made any inner vows in response to fear (statements like, "I'll never trust a man again," or "I'll never

leave the country again," or "I'll never have a close friend again")? When we make inner vows, we create an idol out of our own perspective. We preemptively decide not to trust God and take control of our own story. Ask the Lord if you've ever made a misguided inner vow. If something comes to mind, name it, repent of it, renounce it, and welcome God's cleansing forgiveness. Ask Him to give you a fresh promise for that part of your story. Make space for hope, faith, and courage.

2. Read 2 Kings 4:18–26 and pay attention to how selective the Shunammite woman was with her information. Why do you suppose she told both her husband and Gehazi that everything was fine?

3. Read 2 Kings 4:27–36 and notice how the Shunammite woman sought Elisha's help. She wanted his input in her story because he was the one who first prophesied the promise. This serves as a reminder that problems always accompany the promise. Receiving what we desire is never the conclusion of the story. We'll still face trials, and we have an adversary who loves to steal, kill, and destroy. What kind of challenges have accompanied some of your fulfilled promises?

4. Read 2 Kings 5 and notice how Gehazi's true character was revealed. Could it be that the Shunammite woman discerned his duplicity? When we're walking out our promises and when we're facing our fears, we have to be very selective about who we confide in. Not everyone will speak life into your story. Not everyone has your best interests at heart. I used to be an

oversharer. By God's grace, I'm becoming a woman of wisdom, discernment, and restraint. Based on your current season, who are your safest, truest people right now? How do they inspire and encourage you?

GROUP REFLECTION QUESTIONS

CHAPTER ONE: LIVING LOVED

1. Share about a time when you felt most loved.

2. What are some of the most meaningful ways people express their love for you?

3. How do you find your footing again when you've been unfairly critiqued or criticized?

4. What do you do to remind yourself of God's great love for you?

5. How has God's love made a difference in your life?

6. What do you need to do to send your roots down deeper into God's love?

CHAPTER TWO: GOD GIVES ME PURPOSE AND POWER

1. Share about a time when you encountered God or sensed His presence in a way that stopped you in your tracks.

2. How did that experience affect you in the days that followed?

3. Pause here and ask God to show you how self-preservation has kept you from some of His blessings. Be comfortable with silence and a time of waiting on God. Share what you feel comfortable sharing.

4. Who do you say Jesus is?

5. Who are you because of who Jesus is? Be bold!

6. How has your sense of identity in Christ changed over the years?

CHAPTER THREE: GOD FILLS ME WITH UNWAVERING FAITH

1. Share about someone whose faith inspires you.

2. Share a time when you didn't back down in a spiritual battle, when you rose up and stood your ground.

3. Consider Marie's story for a second. Godly people get sick and die. Yet some are miraculously healed on this side of heaven.

How comfortable are you with the mystery of God? How willing are you to dare to trust Him with the outcome in the face of opposition?

4. If you're honest, would you say you give up too soon? If so, why do you suppose that is?

5. Share a breakthrough story that inspires you (yours or someone else's).

CHAPTER FOUR: GOD CULTIVATES GOOD FRUIT IN ME

1. What about Joseph's story stands out to you the most?

2. Though we don't get an inside look at how Joseph related to God, we do see the fruit of his walk with God. The Lord was with Joseph. Who in your life clearly walks with God, bears fruit, and seems to enjoy the Lord's favor?

3. Talk about favor versus favoritism for a moment. From your perspective, how are they different?

4. Notice that God's favor doesn't exempt us from suffering. But it does flip the Enemy's plan on its head. Share a time when you saw real fruit coming from your life during a difficult season.

5. How might you live differently if you remembered (and believed) that you're more spiritual than physical?

6. Have someone read Psalm 105:17–22 and share your thoughts on Joseph's journey—the trials and triumphs. How have your battles prepared you for promotion?

CHAPTER FIVE: GOD RESCUES AND RESTORES ME

1. How does Rahab's story affect you and make you feel?
2. What about her story stands out to you the most?
3. Share the most amazing rescue/redemption story you've ever encountered (someone you know or read about).
4. Read Psalm 18 together and explore how this passage shows we can move from victim to victor. What part of this psalm most speaks to you in your current season?
5. What part of your story still feels like it needs restoring?

CHAPTER SIX: GOD STRENGTHENS ME AND MOVES MY MOUNTAINS

1. Consider Jen's story. What would you do if God asked you to humble yourself and persist in showing love to someone who didn't return the affection?
2. What's your Jericho wall? What mountain do you need to move?

3. How has this battle strengthened you? How has it tenderized you?

4. What part of Joshua's story most stands out to you?

5. Have someone read Romans 5:1–11 and share your thoughts about this passage. Talk about how these virtues are being developed in you right now.

6. Join together and ask God to move your mountains and to change you in the process.

CHAPTER SEVEN: GOD OWES ME NOTHING BUT GIVES ME EVERYTHING

1. Job's test is our test. What did you struggle with as you read Job's story? What parts of his story are still hard to understand in light of God's love?

2. Job's test was also his friends' test. And ours. When we see someone walk through unimaginable hardship, we have two choices: to draw near and serve (and love and listen and pray), or stand back and judge, assess, and diagnose. What's your instinctive tendency, and why?

3. Consider Job's friends. They showed some knowledge of truth in some of their words, but they missed the target completely. Do you think most church wounds come from people speaking "truth" in the absence of love? Or is it something else?

4. We're all made for worship. We're created for awe. But when we drift from an awe-filled, grateful perspective, we instinctively look to ourselves more than God. What helps you keep your focus on God? Talk about a time when you shifted your gaze to God and how it impacted your perspective on your trials.

5. Who in your life could use a listening ear and an nonjudgmental friend? Make a note to reach out to them with kindness and generosity.

CHAPTER EIGHT: GOD ALWAYS SPEAKS A BETTER WORD

1. What words from others still speak to you? Consider both encouraging and discouraging words.

2. How has God helped you sort through some of the hurtful things others have said to you?

3. Can you think of a time when God's Word jumped off the page to you? What was the story or the promise? Why do you suppose God highlighted that passage for you?

4. Consider the fact that there is power in our words. Quiet your hearts. Put some instrumental music on. Spend some time waiting on God. Ask Him to give you an encouraging word for someone in the group. Take some time to encourage and pray for one another.

5. Is there a promise God wants you to hold on to during this season of your life? Share your story with the group if you can't think of one. Maybe someone will share one of their favorite promises with you. Keep searching the Scriptures until you find the promise God has for you!

CHAPTER NINE: GOD, THE GREAT PHYSICIAN, HEALS ME

1. Look back at your younger years (either childhood, teen years, or young adult years). Is there a pattern of theft in your life? Ways the Enemy repeatedly stole from you?

2. From where you stand now, how has God healed, redeemed, and restored your life?

3. What in you still needs healing?

4. What part of your story amazes you the most? What has God done that you still can't believe?

5. Do you live with a holy expectancy? Do you contend for the promises of God and run hard after Jesus? Or have you settled into a comfortable, unchallenged existence where you've stopped expecting anything new from God? No condemnation. Share as honestly as you're comfortable.

6. Spend some time praying for each other and ask God to show you where He wants to heal and redeem your story.

CHAPTER TEN: GOD DELIVERS ME FROM ALL MY FEARS

1. What are you afraid of?
2. In what ways do you accommodate your fears?
3. Is there a part of your story (a fear, or longing in your heart) that you're unwilling to talk about? If you're willing, will you share?
4. Have you ever made any misguided inner vows? Promises to yourself in an effort to self-protect?
5. How has God guided, protected, and provided for you?
6. How would you live if you weren't afraid of anything?

ACKNOWLEDGMENTS

No book is ever produced by one person alone. It takes a village. I'm deeply grateful for my people. I'm thankful to God for His grace, which allows me to serve alongside such incredible kingdom friends.

Kyle Olund, thank you for your friendship and your wisdom. I appreciate you and Jill so much.

To Damon Reiss, Caren Wolfe, Brooke Hill, Lauren Ash, Allison Carter, Elizabeth Hawkins, and Madison Baird: Thank you for this opportunity and for helping me share this message of faith and encouragement with many!

To Jenn McNeil and Brooke Hill for your excellent work, great insights, and challenging suggestions. You helped me bring this book to a new level. Thank you.

To Meg Schmidt and Kara Klontz: Thank you for the brilliant, beautiful cover. I gasped when I first saw it.

Steve Laube, thank you for your faithful years of service.

To my sample readers: Lynn, Bonnie, Reagan, Tiffani, Daryl, Tamra, Sandy, Kay, Aminta, Abby, Tami, and Kathy. Thank you for your input! Love and appreciate you!

To Esther, Lynn, and my superhero prayer warriors. You know who you are. May God lavish His goodness on you for how you've stood in the gap for me.

To Scott and Wendy, our amazing mentors and friends. We love and appreciate you both deeply. Thank you for the unwavering love and wisdom you continue to share with us. We can't imagine our lives without you.

To the team at Faith Radio, I absolutely love working with you all each day! You're a dream come true! May God continue to breathe life into our offerings until we reach the ends of the earth with the love of Christ.

To Lisa Jackson. I'm so grateful for you!

To our wild and wonderful extended family. You're my happy place. I love you so much.

To our precious sons, amazing daughters-in-law, and beautiful grandchildren. You're my world. I pray every day that God's love feels more tangible to you than the day before. May we continue to live as ones who are spoken for.

To my amazing, brilliant husband, Kev. With each passing year, I see you pursuing God more deeply and walking with Him more purposefully. Your steady and sturdy walk of faith brings life and strength to our whole family. I couldn't love and appreciate you more. Thank you for the covering you provide for me. Thank you for making God's love visible and tangible. Love you, honey.

To my precious Jesus, my life is wrapped up in Yours. Thank You for saving, healing, and redeeming me in ways I never thought possible. I'm living expectantly for Your soon return. Please breathe life into the words on these pages. Heal broken hearts. Set captives free. Bring prodigals home. And awaken us all to the wonder of Your great love.

Until I see You face-to-face . . .

My precious King,

I offer this gift to You.

Appendix

GOD CALLS YOU TO . . .

KNOW HIM MORE AND MORE

"This is the way to have eternal life—to know you, the only true God, and Jesus Christ, the one you sent to earth."

(JOHN 17:3)

WORSHIP PASSIONATELY

Shout with joy to the LORD, all the earth!
Worship the LORD with gladness.
Come before him, singing with joy.
Acknowledge that the LORD is God!
He made us, and we are his.
We are his people, the sheep of his pasture.
Enter his gates with thanksgiving;
go into his courts with praise.
Give thanks to him and praise his name.
For the LORD is good.
His unfailing love continues forever,
and his faithfulness continues to each generation.

(PSALM 100)

WAIT EAGERLY

Those who trust in the Lord will find new strength.
They will soar high on wings like eagles.
They will run and not grow weary.
They will walk and not faint.

(ISAIAH 40:31)

ABIDE IN HIS WORD

"If you remain in me and my words remain in you, you may ask for anything you want, and it will be granted!"

(JOHN 15:7)

PRAY CONTINUALLY

Always be joyful. Never stop praying.

(1 THESSALONIANS 5:16–17)

BE THANKFUL

Be thankful in all circumstances, for this is God's will for you who belong to Christ Jesus.

(1 THESSALONIANS 5:18)

HOLINESS

The Scriptures say, "You must be holy because I am holy."

(1 PETER 1:16)

GODLY COMMUNITY

Let us think of ways to motivate one another to acts of love and good works. And let us not neglect our meeting together, as some people do, but encourage one another, especially now that the day of his return is drawing near.

(HEBREWS 10:24–25)

WISE STEWARDSHIP

The Lord replied, "A faithful, sensible servant is one to whom the master can give the responsibility of managing his other household servants and feeding them. If the master returns and finds that the servant has done a good job, there will be a reward. I tell you the truth, the master will put that servant in charge of all he owns."

(LUKE 12:42–44)

HUMILITY

Humble yourselves under the mighty power of God, and at the right time he will lift you up in honor.

(1 PETER 5:6)

GIVE AND RECEIVE FORGIVENESS

Get rid of all bitterness, rage, anger, harsh words, and slander, as well as all types of evil behavior. Instead, be kind to each other, tenderhearted, forgiving one another, just as God through Christ has forgiven you.

(EPHESIANS 4:31–32)

TAKE AUTHORITY OVER THE POWER OF THE ENEMY

"I have given you authority over all the power of the enemy, and you can walk among snakes and scorpions and crush them. Nothing will injure you."

(LUKE 10:19)

SHINE

"You are the light of the world—like a city on a hilltop that cannot be hidden. No one lights a lamp and then puts it under a basket. Instead, a lamp is placed on a stand, where it gives light to everyone in the house. In the same way, let your good deeds shine out for all to see, so that everyone will praise your heavenly Father."

(MATTHEW 5:14–16)

DO GOOD WORK

We are God's masterpiece. He has created us anew in Christ Jesus, so we can do the good things he planned for us long ago.

(EPHESIANS 2:10)

SHARE JESUS

Then he told them, "Go into all the world and preach the Good News to everyone."

(MARK 16:15)

OBEY

Peter and the apostles replied, "We must obey God rather than any human authority."

(ACTS 5:29)

GROW IN LOVE

May you have the power to understand, as all God's people should, how wide, how long, how high, and how deep his love is. May you experience the love of Christ, though it is too great to understand fully. Then you will be made complete with all the fullness of life and power that comes from God.

(EPHESIANS 3:18–19)

JOY

The Holy Spirit produces this kind of fruit in our lives: love, joy, peace, patience, kindness, goodness, faithfulness, gentleness, and self-control. There is no law against these things!

(GALATIANS 5:22–23)

PEACE

You will keep in perfect peace
all who trust in you,
all whose thoughts are fixed on you!

(ISAIAH 26:3)

PATIENCE

Love is patient and kind. Love is not jealous or boastful or proud or rude. It does not demand its own way. It is not irritable, and it keeps no record of being wronged.

(1 CORINTHIANS 13:4–5)

KINDNESS

Be kind to each other, tenderhearted, forgiving one another, just as God through Christ has forgiven you.

(EPHESIANS 4:32)

GENTLENESS

Let your gentleness be evident to all. The Lord is near.

(PHILIPPIANS 4:5 NIV)

FAITHFULNESS

"If you are faithful in little things, you will be faithful in large ones. But if you are dishonest in little things, you won't be honest with greater responsibilities."

(LUKE 16:10)

GOODNESS

Taste and see that the LORD is good.
Oh, the joys of those who take refuge in him!

(PSALM 34:8)

SELF-CONTROL

Better to be patient than powerful;
better to have self-control than to conquer a city.

(PROVERBS 16:32)

SURRENDER

Trust in the LORD with all your heart;
do not depend on your own understanding.

Seek his will in all you do,
and he will show you which path to take.

(PROVERBS 3:5-6)

PERSEVERE AND ENDURE

Do not throw away this confident trust in the Lord. Remember the great reward it brings you! Patient endurance is what you need now, so that you will continue to do God's will. Then you will receive all that he has promised.

(HEBREWS 10:35-36)

FAST

"When you fast, don't make it obvious, as the hypocrites do, for they try to look miserable and disheveled so people will admire them for their fasting. I tell you the truth, that is the only reward they will ever get. But when you fast, comb your hair and wash your face. Then no one will notice that you are fasting, except your Father, who knows what you do in private. And your Father, who sees everything, will reward you."

(MATTHEW 6:16-18)

FAITH

Faith shows the reality of what we hope for; it is the evidence of things we cannot see. Through their faith, the people in days of old earned a good reputation. By faith we understand that the entire universe was formed at God's command, that what we now see did not come from anything that can be seen.

(HEBREWS 11:1-3)

HOPE

Let us hold tightly without wavering to the hope we affirm, for God can be trusted to keep his promise.

(HEBREWS 10:23)

COURAGE

"This is my command—be strong and courageous! Do not be afraid or discouraged. For the Lord your God is with you wherever you go."

(JOSHUA 1:9)

STRENGTH

A final word: Be strong in the Lord and in his mighty power.

(EPHESIANS 6:10)

RENEW YOUR MIND

Don't copy the behavior and customs of this world, but let God transform you into a new person by changing the way you think. Then you will learn to know God's will for you, which is good and pleasing and perfect.

(ROMANS 12:2)

DIVINE STRATEGY IN EVERY SITUATION

Your own ears will hear him.
Right behind you a voice will say,
"This is the way you should go,"
whether to the right or to the left.

(ISAIAH 30:21)

PROCLAIM HIS POWER AND GOODNESS

All of your works will thank you, Lord,
and your faithful followers will praise you.
They will speak of the glory of your kingdom;
they will give examples of your power.

(PSALM 145:10–11)

LISTEN AND UNDERSTAND

"When the Father sends the Advocate as my representative—that is, the Holy Spirit—he will teach you everything and will remind you of everything I have told you."

(JOHN 14:26)

LIVE WITH ETERNITY IN MIND

We don't look at the troubles we can see now; rather, we fix our gaze on things that cannot be seen. For the things we see now will soon be gone, but the things we cannot see will last forever.

(2 CORINTHIANS 4:18)

SUBMIT TO GOD AND RESIST THE DEVIL

Humble yourselves before God. Resist the devil, and he will flee from you.

(JAMES 4:7)

FLEE TEMPTATION

Run from anything that stimulates youthful lusts. Instead, pursue righteous living, faithfulness, love, and peace. Enjoy the companionship of those who call on the Lord with pure hearts.

(2 TIMOTHY 2:22)

GIVE GENEROUSLY

God is the one who provides seed for the farmer and then bread to eat. In the same way, he will provide and increase your resources and then produce a great harvest of generosity in you. Yes, you will be enriched in every way so that you can always be generous.

(2 CORINTHIANS 9:10–11)

HELP THE POOR

If you help the poor, you are lending to the LORD—
and he will repay you!

(PROVERBS 19:17)

LIVE WISELY

Teach us to number our days,
that we may gain a heart of wisdom.

(PSALM 90:12 NIV)

TAKE RISKS

So you see, faith by itself isn't enough. Unless it produces good deeds, it is dead and useless.

(JAMES 2:17)

ASK, SEEK, AND KNOCK

"Keep on asking, and you will receive what you ask for. Keep on seeking, and you will find. Keep on knocking, and the door will be opened to you. For everyone who asks, receives. Everyone who seeks, finds. And to everyone who knocks, the door will be opened."

(MATTHEW 7:7–8)

FINISH WELL

All glory to God, who is able to keep you from falling away and will bring you with great joy into his glorious presence without a single fault. All glory to him who alone is God, our Savior through Jesus Christ our Lord. All glory, majesty, power, and authority are his before all time, and in the present, and beyond all time! Amen.

(JUDE VV. 24–25)

NOTES

CHAPTER 1

1. A. W. Tozer, *The Pursuit of God*, ed. James L. Snyder (Bethany House, 2013), 54.

CHAPTER 2

1. Lenny LeBlanc, "There Is None Like You," track 13 on *Pure Heart*, Integrity Music, 1991.
2. Ann Voskamp, *Loved to Life: A 40-Day Pilgrimage with Love Himself That Will Change Your Life* (Tyndale Momentum, 2025), 22–23.
3. Dr. Rob Reimer, *Soul Care: Seven Transformational Principles for a Healthy Soul* (Carpenter's Son, 2016), 38–39.
4. Dr. Saundra Dalton-Smith, *Being Fully Known: The Joyful Satisfaction of Beholding, Becoming, and Belonging* (Esther Press, 2025), 80.

CHAPTER 3

1. Sharon Hodde Miller, *The Cost of Control: Why We Crave It, the Anxiety It Gives Us, and the Real Power God Promises* (Baker Books, 2022), 71.
2. This account is my creative paraphrase of the scene from 2 Kings 4:1–7.
3. Chip Ingram joined me on *Susie Larson Live* on June 4, 2025, to talk about his book *I Choose Joy*. This is my paraphrase of what he said on the show.

CHAPTER 4

1. Tessa Afshar, *The Rested Soul: 30 Meditations to Quiet Your Heart* (Moody Publishers, 2024), 128.

CHAPTER 5

1. L. B. Cowman, *Streams in the Desert: 366 Daily Devotional Readings*, ed. Jim Reimann (Zondervan, 2013), 223.
2. Warren W. Wiersbe, *The Wiersbe Bible Commentary: Old Testament* (David C Cook, 2007), 385.
3. Sheila Walsh, *Holding On When You Want to Let Go: Clinging to Hope When Life Is Falling Apart* (Baker Books, 2021), 152.

CHAPTER 6

1. Tim Timberlake, *The Art of Overcoming: Letting God Turn Your Endings into Beginnings* (W Publishing, 2023), 170.
2. Adapted from Susie Larson, *Prevail: 365 Days of Enduring Strength from God's Word* (Bethany House, 2020), 51.
3. Randall Price and H. Wayne House, *Zondervan Handbook of Biblical Archaeology: A Book by Book Guide to Archaeological Discoveries Related to the Bible* (Zondervan Academic, 2017), 107.
4. Mark Batterson, *Draw the Circle: The 40 Day Prayer Challenge* (Zondervan, 2012), 93.

CHAPTER 7

1. Adapted from Susie Larson, *Closer Than Your Next Breath: Where Is God When You Need Him Most?* (W Publishing, 2023), 62–63.
2. This is my paraphrase of Otto Koning's story as found in a sermon he delivered. Otto Koning, "The Pineapple Story | Otto Koning," sermon, posted April 29, 2025, by Institute in Basic Life Principles, YouTube, https://youtu.be/VKYl6OM_eN0?si=K0dpeRNgH6HVlhMq.
3. Samuel Rodriguez, *Fresh Oil, Holy Fire, New Wine: Living the Vibrant Holy Spirit-Filled Life* (Chosen Books, 2024), 98–99, emphasis mine.

CHAPTER 8

1. Joby Martin and Charles Martin, *Anything Is Possible: How Nine Miracles of Jesus Reveal God's Love for You* (FaithWords, 2023), 218–19.

CHAPTER 9

1. See Joel 3:10, NKJV.
2. Mark Fischetti and Jen Christiansen, "Our Bodies Replace Billions of Cells Every Day," *Scientific American*, April 1, 2021, https://www.scientificamerican.com/article/our-bodies-replace-billions-of-cells-every-day/.
3. The following is my paraphrase and interpretation of the story of the woman with the issue of blood. You can find her story in Matthew 9:20–22, Mark 5:24–34, and Luke 8:42–48.
4. StudyLight.org, Interlinear Bible Search, "Luke 8:48: thygátēr," accessed November 17, 2025, https://studylight.org/study-desk/interlinear.html?q1=luke+8%3A48.
5. Dr. Saundra Dalton-Smith, *Being Fully Known: The Joyful Satisfaction of Beholding, Becoming, and Belonging* (Esther Press, 2025), 80.

CHAPTER 10

1. Here are a few verses on inquiring of the Lord: 1 Samuel 23:2; Psalm 34:4–17; Isaiah 55:6–7; Jeremiah 10:21, 33:3.
2. Jamie Winship, *Living Fearless: Exchanging the Lies of the World for the Liberating Truth of God* (Revell, 2022), 80–81, emphasis mine.
3. I tell this story in my book *Waking Up to the Goodness of God: 40 Days Toward Healing & Wholeness* (Thomas Nelson, 2024), 106.

ABOUT THE AUTHOR

Susie Larson is a well-known radio talk show host and podcaster with over 16 million downloads, a national speaker, and a bestselling author. She has written twenty-three books and is a seasoned veteran in the fitness industry. She has been recognized twice as a top-ten finalist for the John C. Maxwell Transformational Leadership Award. Susie and her husband live near Minneapolis with their three sons, three daughters-in-law, and a growing number of delightful grandchildren. Her passion is to inspire people everywhere to recognize the value of their soul, the depth of God's love, and the height of their calling in Christ Jesus.